Flying the Glass Airplane
Poetry From My Extraordinary Ordinary Life

Linda Katz Buckbinder

www.highpointpubs.com

Copyright © 2025 by Linda Katz Buckbinder

All rights reserved. Published in the United States of America. No part of this book may be reproduced or transmitted in any form or by any means, graphic, electronic or mechanical, including photocopying, recording, taping or by any information storage or retrieval system, without permission in writing from the publisher.

This edition published by Highpoint Lit
For information, write to info@highpointpubs.com.
First Edition
ISBN: 979-8-9908488-8-7

Library of Congress Cataloging-in-Publication Data
Buckbinder, Linda
Flying the Glass Airplane
Poetry From My Extraordinary Ordinary Life

Summary: "This soaring collection of poetry reveals the beauty and wonder in everyday living and a multifaceted life well-lived."
– Provided by publisher.

ISBN: 979-8-9908488-8-7 (paperback)
1. Poetry

Library of Congress Control Number: 2025905639

Cover art by Linda Katz Buckbinder, "Self Portrait"
Book design by Sarah M. Clarehart

Manufactured in the United States of America

Dedication/Acknowledgements

This book is dedicated
to that long-ago day when you came into my life,
and the day, some years later, when I truly realized that I had discovered
Gold.

To my Endless Love,
David

I would like to thank Michael Roney, friend and publisher, for making this
dream come true,
and for his kindness, knowledge, and patience.
I am forever grateful.

A special thank you to the talented Sarah Clarehart for her wonderful work
on design and layout for my book.

Special thanks to my dear friend, Marilyn Keizer, for her gentle coaxing,
to convince me that I should put my poetry out in the world.

Here I am, World!

Contents

Musings I
My Ordinary Life....2
Gathering Up the Light....3
Alive....5
Eyes....7
Winter Morning....9
The Heart of a Dog....10
Empath?....12
Ray....14
On Painting a Self-Portrait....16
Ocean in Winter....18

Elections, Pandemics, and Miracles
A Chilly Morning....20
Bird....22
The Doves....24
The First Time I heard Tal Play Barber's Adagio for Strings....26
Through the Curtain of Darkness....28
On Holding an Infant....30
Walking in the Pool....32
Connections....34
Butterflies....36
Connecting With My Parents....38
I Dreamed We Could Hug Again....40
Sunset....42

Ancient History
Best Friends....44
Finding the Child Within....46
First Love....48
GH....49
Safety....51
Spring....53
When I Remember You....54
The Quest for Love....56
Hungarian Food....58
This Place....60
Hiking with Dogs....62

Family
Family....66
We had a Station Wagon....68
Photographs of My Mother....70
Garage Sale....72
My Father's Voice....74
My Father's Death....75
Visiting My Parents' Graves 77
Restaurant Reflections....78
LBI and the Katz Family....80

Watching Tal Grow
Before Dawn....84
You Will Be Thirty In A Few Months....86
Talya is "Dew from Heaven" in Hebrew....87
Talia, Part 1....89
Talia, Part 2 91
"An Unusual Child"....91
The Cats....94
The Most Glorious of Songs....96
Still Learning about Love....98
Rescue....100
Conversation with my Daughter....102

My Endless Love
Davie's Birthday....106
Forty-One Years Later....108
Just the Two of Us....110
Love Story....112
Sleep Partners....114

Arizona
Wind Chimes....118
Wildness....120
What Makes Me Feel Safe....122
Hummingbird....124
Thrive....126
The Common Good....128
Like the Songbirds....130
The Little Orange Tree....132

Musings 2
Who Would I Be....136
In the Light of Day....138
Thoughts on Flying....139
The Stars....141
A Poet Walks Into a Bar.......143
Your Old Eyes....146
Visiting Donna's Art....147
Mermaid Reflections....149
Change....151
Music that Fills my Day....153

Musings I

My Ordinary Life

Woke up this morning to a rare day in Arizona,
The sky an abstract of aqua with indigo swirls,
the air thick with moisture, blues heavy with grey,
greens deeper, voluptuous,

Sliding shadows of clouds mirrored in the rain-slick streets,
Silvery sky reflected in puddles on the patio.

How often do I look around me and think of paintings?
How often do I take my morning walk, in a trance,
Surrounded by exquisite beauty,
Comparing what I see to Cezanne, Innes, or Constable?
When these glorious paintings pale in comparison
to the ordinary life I am living.

Art has brought me closer to life, colors richer, juicier.
With every step I take,
I experience yet another brilliant composition of line and space,
textures I feel without touching,
a palette of colors with and without names,
a dazzling cornucopia of gorgeous.
I am inspired to paint and write,
but how can I ever translate this sensual exploration
into a painting or poem?

For the more intimate I am with my world,
the more I know I can never reproduce or improve on it
with pen or brush.

And so, I do not try, but humbly dance in the sunlight,
Dream in the valley of the violet mountains,
Laugh with joy at my ordinary life,
and pour my heart into another painting,
another poem.

Gathering Up the Light

I linger in bed,
recalling bits and pieces of dreams,
floating in that last sliver of slumber
disappearing like a whisp of smoke.
I would stay and savor the warm hug
but is there anything better in this life than
breakfast?
The smell of pancakes on the buttered griddle,
Sweet, sticky maple syrup drizzled,
strawberries languishing on the side.
Steaming coffee nudging my energy to the foreground,
well worth pushing off the covers.

Sound the trumpets! Proclaim the new day!
Behold the spectacular sunrise that bleeds crimson, behind silhouettes
of pineapple palms and deep violet mountains
rewriting the night
into morning
with a flourish!

I am lighter than the luminous morning air
as I walk by the little yellow flowers
preferred by the hummingbirds,
the orange jubilee and the purple sage,
the oleander bushes with their pink wreaths.

I am earnestly gathering light,
I find it in the smiles of my neighbors, waving to me as they
take out the garbage.
I see a frail, bent man,
one hand on his walker
and one hand gently stroking a friend's wriggling black lab,
a pail of freshly picked oranges left at the end of a driveway
for passersby.

Everywhere there is light
and I, like a child gathering wildflowers for a bouquet,
gather up the light of this new day.

I must bring it home for the times when I am
gray with hopelessness
to place in a prominent corner of my heart,
for the times I can see no hint of kindness in the world

for this is a lie

I am gathering light to illuminate the darkness
for the days when I forget
that I am
we are
all
light.

Alive

I was already alive for a long time before I was aware of being alive,
so when I finally thought about it, I felt like I'd missed something.

But I already had picked blackberries in the blazing August sun,
piercing my fingers with purple blood
and skinned my knees trying to climb the
big rock in the gully

I was way past sucking the nectar from the honeysuckle flowers
with my best
friends in our secret place,
pretending we were spies,

Years past my first crush on a boy who almost walked through me,
I was so invisible.

Maybe even past my first "love" in high school,
the boy who played flute and had huge brown eyes that followed me
everywhere.
I can't tell you the exact moment that I realized,
truly realized, that I was alive,

because I think it crept up on me slowly. I think it was retroactive though.
I mean,
looking back, I was even more alive before I knew what it meant to be alive.
When I finally started to think about it, it may have disappeared a little.
You don't do "alive" by thinking. You do it by quieting your thoughts,
by being.
By leaving the past and the future and entering the present moment.

Being alive isn't just being happy either. It's what you feel without
thinking at all.
It's the electricity in your love, the chemistry in your relationships,
the gratitude and awe in your heart, the sadness, the mystery in living and
dying.

The everyday miracles, the successes and the losses.

It's the little things: watching a ladybug on a blade of grass,
the fatigue in your arm muscles when you have been kneading
dough for ten minutes,
the way your palms sting after you have been clapping hard for a great
performance,
the spontaneous smile of a child
that takes your breath away,

the moment you wake up out of your head
and into your heart.

Eyes

I never paint eyes first
They have the final say
They pull the portrait together
with personality,
with intention,
meaning.

When I first met my husband,
I saw him from the side, the back, in motion.
When he looked at me
I saw nothing but those eyes
I think he was talking to me, but I wasn't listening.
Those eyes!
not lavender
or two different colors
or large with long lashes
just an instant connection
that rendered me breathless.

a portal into the future perhaps?

When my daughter was a baby,
her eyes were too big for her face
hands too small to grasp the world
but hungry eyes that devoured it.

What I see when I look out the picture window
depends on my life in that moment.

The sunrise can appear as a wash of sparkling orange gold
over the oleander leaves
bringing with it glorious possibilities,
or it can be what wakes me up from my much-coveted sleep
too soon.

The lean coyote can appear as a starving predator or
a miracle of creation, intent on survival.

My eyes translate what I see into my unique story
and then my story creates what I see.

I am endlessly grateful for my eyes,
They remind me that it is not so much what I see
but what I can envision with love
that matters.

Winter Morning

I open my eyes slowly,
reach out to feel Davey's empty place next to me,
disappointed,
I stretch like a cat, as muscles, bones, joints come to life,
like Pinocchio transforming from wood to flesh,
I breathe into the new day.

My mother kept the heat at 55 degrees at night.
On winter mornings growing up, I sat crouched
in a ball by the heat vent,
eating Frosted Cornflakes and milk,
Comforted by the warmth and smell of the heat,
until I could turn out to the cold, in my grown-up school clothes,
face the distance between my family's embrace and the world
that threatened to swallow me,
or spit me out, mangled.

At lunchtime, I flew over the sidewalk cracks, past the dentist's office,
down the hill to the cul-de-sac,
Gooey grilled cheese sandwich and minestrone soup waiting for me,
My mother, welcoming me into her kitchen of garlic and potato
smells,
and that steady, glowing light.

Today, I dress in my grown-up clothes slowly, luxuriously,
Looking for the warmth, staying in the shower a little too long.
I haven't quite crossed over into my persona yet: professional,
social,
moderating and mediating,
measuring words, calculating responses....

My breath is visible, but a dream refuses to dissipate
as I drive to work.

The Heart of a Dog

Every morning, it is my birthday!
I wake up to the new day, rip off the vestiges of
tattered dreams and nonsensical nostalgia
like wrapping paper,
like the tangled covers of my bed,
anxious to jump into solid reality,
or at least greet myself in the mirror,
acknowledge my aging body, my faltering mind,
but also
smile,
Happy Birthday!

For all my flaws,
in me beats
the heart of a dog,
as I exuberantly greet the new day
as if I am Alive
for the first time,
with unbounded joy,
nearly drooling with glee
at the stars fading into the light
like waves fading into the ocean,
the penetrating depth of silence
that exists in the desert before dawn,
the exquisite breeze that heralds
the perfect day.

I have always led with my heart.

I am a puzzle with pieces lost along the journey,
maybe too long ago
before I was aware of the goodness of
my gentle heart.

I suppose I am someone

who sometimes doesn't feel quite
enough

But I trust my heart,
more than my memory
more than my reasoning
more than any intention for kindness

The heart of a dog
loves deeply and gives wholly,
unaware of its own
Gold.

Empath?

I have not slept through the night since my twenties.
I get hot and cold, covers off, covers on.
Legs hanging off the bed,
curled up with one arm over my head or hanging on to Davie.
I can't get comfortable in my body or my bed.

My pillow is not my friend.
I grasp it like a life jacket—a personal flotation
device.
Now it is 2 a.m., and I can't get back to sleep.

As an infant, Talia kept us up most of the night.
As she grew to be a toddler, she insisted that I sing to her —
the same songs over and over, all night long.
My fault—I sang to her in
the womb, so she assumed I could just keep serenading
into her terrible twos.

Ragged and sleep deprived, my mother offered,
"You have thirty minutes, go take a nap. I will watch the baby."
Being on the clock just makes it worse.

Ever hear of the Princess and the Pea?
That's me.
I love my soft, warm, cozy slippers. I wear
them whenever I am in my house, in lieu of shoes.
For the past few weeks, I felt a pain in my left foot.
Finally, instead of heading for the doctor's office, I looked
at the bottom of the slipper,
a plastic piece was sticking into the slipper
and piercing through to my foot.

My sensitivity knows no boundaries. I am prone to crying at the
drop of a hat.

A friend of mine recently said to me, "Have you ever considered that you might be an empath?"

Sometimes I get a thought, and it won't leave, no matter how nicely I ask.
I know I am not alone in this. It's difficult, right?
I recommend meditation, soothing thoughts, smiling at yourself in the mirror,
prayers, reading an exhilarating book. Taking a walk in Nature.
Possibly a small glass of wine.

Anything that works.

Ray

Rui (Ray) is going to redo our guest bathroom.
She is half an hour late for our meeting.
This morning, she had blood drawn.
Ray is thin like me, and we both have issues with phlebotomists.
She shows me her arm, and the blue gauze around it.
In her heavy Mandarin accent, she says,
"Woman treat me like a child, ask what color gauze I want."

Ray is the coolest contractor I have met out here, maybe anywhere.
No nonsense, brutally and fully honest, charming, but straight
to the point,
and usually right on time.

I met her last year, when she did our master bath.
She lives in a rural area of Surprise, in a massive stone home on a
sweeping property, with fruit vines and horses.

We roamed around outside,
looking at stones for our countertop. This time though, we tell her
what we want, no need to drive out,
though I wouldn't have minded revisiting that
vast, idyllic property.

This morning, we sit down at the table to sign off on the work.
Ray tells us about her family in Beijing.
Her father is 93,
She visited her family last summer.
Her father is doing ok now, but there is already bickering
among the sisters about the will…

Rai is disgusted. She tells her parents she wants nothing to do with
the arguing and backstabbing.
"Keep your money, I don't need," she says.
She is disappointed, and I see it in her expression, in
the look on her face.

I tell her, "All will return to love in due time."
This is a common issue for families," I say.
I remember all that came up when my parents died.
Everyone is grieving and they are looking to hold on to the past
and make sense of Death.
Now, my siblings and I have regrown
our relationships, they are stronger, more resilient.

I think now we are closer than ever.

On Painting a Self-Portrait

Well, here are a bunch of photos of me that I can use:
Here I am years ago; it was taken in the backyard
by Noam, a friend of the family,
excellent photographer.
I am leaning against a tree
What am I wearing? Is that a bathing suit?
Oh my.
Not much coverage....

Ok, here's one of me in a professional headshot when I was a
working musician.
Very flirtatious, come-hither look, I think.
Not so much sexual as, "hire me please"
Or maybe it is sort of sexual...
and definitely not representative of me today.

And what about these poses with boyfriends over the years.
Not bad, I guess, but vacuous,
vacant. Missing something important:
who I really am.

So, I am standing in front of the bathroom mirror.
I do that quite frequently these days.
The years have etched unwanted lines on my face and
bags under my eyes. I cringe.

In a moment of clarity, I choose to push the vanity aside.
This isn't about looking young and
beautiful.

Now, it's about being authentically me.
True to myself.
I am alive, living an ordinary life,
Proud of my accomplishments and proud of who I have
become:

a life of love, strength, compassion, learning, growing, failure,
victories,
a product of joy and hardship,
relationships that blossomed and
relationships that petered out.
proud of my heart,

I look forward to every moment of
every day—a gift. I do not take this miracle of life for granted.

Happy to greet the sunrise, to see the hummingbirds outside my window,
flitting about the flowers on the orange jubilee.

I pull out the stretched paper and the paints. I smile.
This is going to be a poem
without words.

Ocean in Winter

Long past the crowds of sleek-skinned swimmers,
Children calling against the wind to brothers and sisters, "bring more sand for the castle!"
Strolling couples holding hands as their ankles sink into the wet apron of the waves,

Sound bites from portable speakers and snippets of laughter,
air rich with sunscreen, salt, and fish
and the waves, dressed in droplets of gold.

Now, in winter, I walk along the water's edge, the pale grey sky sinking into the ocean at the horizon.

The sounds are different.
I hear the birds, fishing and foraging,

Then the wind, which is lashing against my windbreaker,
My hair flying in my eyes, in my mouth.
But the loudest sound of all
is the ocean itself,
frolicking, laughing, raging, crying

The personality of this place has changed,
muted from its bright
summer colors,
There is a serenity
But there is also a joyous coming home
to the truth of this grand tableau:

It is an Impressionist painting,

shades of blues, grays, greens, browns and violets,
accented by strokes of white, dynamic and ever moving,
melding, to create an ongoing masterpiece without an end
That, in this wintry season,
only a few

come to witness.

Elections, Pandemics, and Miracles

A Chilly Morning

It is late for my morning walk—5:45 a.m.
Yet still and breathless
in the shadows of the tall palms and
palo verde trees.
Surprisingly, no one is about.
Where are the dog walkers this morning?
Where is the buff guy who wears a sleeveless shirt and
carries two large weights in his hands as he walks?

I look up to smile at the spectacular stars,
preening, grandstanding, winking
in their cerulean sea.
As always, I am charmed.

It is forty-one degrees, chilly for Arizona,
I secure my scarf around my neck, walk a little faster,
and stuff my hands in my pockets

remembering that,
Yes, today is October 31, Halloween!
I look around,
houses dark and silent,
no Halloween decorations to amuse me.

Halloween is my thirty-three-year-old daughter's favorite holiday.
 A perennial child, she takes it quite seriously,
still wears outlandish costumes with red contact lenses
and fake fangs.

The silly skeletons, scary witches and ghosts, and lit up pumpkins have been replaced
by election signs,
serious business,
the fun and whimsy of the season left in boxes and
bags in the garage.

But the election is far spookier than any of those decorations.
Though not in a good way:
It has drained the life out of our community

Leaving behind fear, anger, exhaustion.

When it is finally over,
perhaps we can have a redo
of Halloween.

Bird

I was walking in the neighborhood
as I often do on comfortable summer mornings,
when the world belongs to early risers—
the birds and the bunnies,
the velvety morning glory
the dew-topped grass in the park.

It is most pleasant when my thoughts
do not push in,
when I am left to simply feel
and linger in the voluptuous beauty,
the glory
of the new day.

When run-away thoughts ambush me,
I am in some rehearsal of conversation
or explanation,
in the grip of remorse,
shame,
regret,
judgement.

On this day,
a bird swooped down from a tree
as in a Hitchcock movie,
squawked angrily,
chased me up the street.
I stopped at the top of the hill,
Breathless.

and then I laughed until I doubled over with…
Awareness!

that this feisty creature
was no monster or nightmare,

but had awakened me
from one

for in my dream,
I forgot
to trust
who I really am.

The Doves

I am walking amidst the throbbing intensity of colors,
The smells of the orange blossoms and the honeysuckle bushes
the cacophony of birdsong,
the life below my feet,
and the life hiding amidst the bougainvillea
and the oleanders

the hares and the coyotes

In the developing dawn,
the quail family waddles past in a row
like Madeline and the little French girls,

a bobcat slinks across the street

The beauty that calls to me to open my heart,
shed my old skin,
and be born anew.

While in the world there is this horror that looms,
that steals my breath and renders it shallow
An undertow of fear that pulls at my feet
even as I breathe in the delicious smell of desert spring
and delight in the warmth of the sun on my shoulders.

I turn my gaze to the small wonders of my world,
to my ordinary life.
I look inside me for the breath that buoys me, for the alchemy that will transform fear into peace,
The realization that there is a river that runs through us all and the hope that, once we discover this,
it will bring us closer to one another.

I am home, looking out the window as I type.
And here are the doves,

I like to watch them come together
atop the columns in the backyard,
always snuggling, cuddling, cooing.

Suddenly,
to my horror,
a falcon has one of the doves,
swoops it off the column and they fly into the glass,

a struggle for life…

The dove dead
and the falcon gone, dazed.

I wipe a tear from my eye.

The next morning a lone dove sits on the column,
searching for its mate,
Waiting

Life disappears in a brutal moment,
unexpected, without warning.

There is no choice, I think.
Change is inevitable,
Change or change will happen without your permission.

I am in awe of the rainbow,
though I know it will not last the hour.

Mostly, I cling to the present moment.
It is all we have.
It is here in this moment that all is alive,
I bask in its glory
I am immersed in gratitude.

It is all we have.

The First Time I heard Tal Play Barber's Adagio for Strings

She was performing with a NY ensemble.
I couldn't have been more unprepared.
The piece started slowly, with a great, deepening feeling.
My eyes closed, I wanted to be fully
embraced, held.
I floated up, into an awakening sky,
my heart beating like the wings of a dove.

my eyes opened to a pulsating light,
Surrounded by playful blue-eyed angels in diaphanous
robes, holding sweet-smelling bouquets
of full-lipped white roses
and smiling peonies,
every sense in my body aroused.

then the final ascent,
the strings intensifying in a powerful, unified voice,
a deepening,
accelerating growing of my life
from child to adult to angel—
my breath quickening,
on my way toward a glowing, golden light,
Eternity.

And just when my euphoria bloomed fully,
I exhaled, and
began to fall back to Earth, a controlled,
silvery descent,
the poignant denouement
of a glorious piece of music.

When my eyes opened, tears slid down
glistening cheeks.

The cheers of the audience battered the tenderness left in my heart
I stayed in my seat until they closed the hall.
etching the moment
into my soul.

Through the Curtain of Darkness

My walks are sandwiched between
blinking stars
in the late-night sky
and the sliver of light
that is dawn,

the birds not yet mingling,
the palpable quiet,
The day readying to rise
as shards of light already peak through
the curtain of darkness

and Nature's audience awaits,
without expectation
of anything new,

the repeat performance
of the Glorious Sunrise.

And I, fussing with my phone,
my mind filled with thoughts of little importance,
stop suddenly
there on the sidewalk,
holding my breath,
A very young coyote
Looked up at me
for only a few heartbeats.

Then I noticed that it was not alone.

The coyote bowed his head and sniffed a small rabbit
who was lazily exploring the sidewalk,
and there they stood,
for what seemed like eternity,
sniffing one another and doing nothing

but sharing company
in the gray light.

At some point, I turned around and
walked the other way,
attempting to process
this odd behavior of hunter and prey
in a world of caste and hierarchy
in a world of rules
needing to be broken,
or not.

On Holding an Infant

I breathe in her earthy smell of sleep
She is wrapped in a wool blanket
like a warm loaf of bread
tiny fingers searching, grabbing at the air
trying to hold onto something,
What?

eyes adjusting to the glare of the world,
half-closed
she sees light and dark,
knows her mother's song
more than her own.

Do you remember when life was simple?
when you were bundled safely in loving arms
dancing to the heartbeat of a living God
feeling the breath around you
delicate on your body
basking in the glow of ancient dreams
and rocking gently in a golden moment
you had no way of knowing
would not last.

Holding this infant
will hasten her change from angel to human,
a joint humanity of beating hearts,
like the one she is sensing
and in turn,
softening

a deep connection to Life
and to other,
awakening as I hold her

wanting to stay here in this moment for her,

before life becomes a labyrinth of paths taken
and not taken,
choices that will conceive joy
or regret
possibilities that will blossom
or wither.

But in this moment
in this heartbeat,

Everything exists.

Walking in the Pool

Billie and I walk in the pool.

The water is meant to relax me,
yet I shiver from the cold, or maybe it's the stress
of the election.

a woman and a man are arguing loudly about
this very subject
she storms out of the pool,
a sour look on her face.

I am not alone in this.
The country seems to be flailing,
anger and fear and sadness
and hope—
 the smell and sound that
permeates everything,
like roses and garbage.

I talk to Billie in hushed tones
about living each day with tears so close to the surface
I can taste them
At times, my eyes fill with tears
for seemingly no reason.

But Billie makes me laugh
She is a brilliant artist
navigating life
with a soft touch and a loving heart,
Humor and calm
and perspective,
that comes from living
with deep commitment
and deep trust.

She paints a dazzling picture of the world,
as ugly as it now seems to me,
It is beautiful to Billie
Gorgeous color and pleasing shapes,
Inspiration for the suffering.

It's just the two of us in the pool now
I want to stay here
Laughing, telling stories, moving my arms and legs
vigorously in the water.

Connections

After my mother died,
I found pennies
most mornings on my walk,
in the woods
or on the street.

I felt her presence and her love.
Sometimes it was an answer to a question
my heart was pondering
Sometimes it was her way of letting me know
she was with me.

The small plant in the kitchen I water and tend to
with devotion and care
a gift from a dear friend,
its swelling green presence
reminding me daily
of her warm smile,
time spent together.

In all of us is the seed of connection
waiting to be nurtured
I saw it in the tiny, brazen child who grabbed my hand in the park
and pulled me into her dance of joy.

She awakened something deep in my soul--
the stirring of the seed
after a long year of disconnect

and in my friends and neighbors who received the virus vaccine,
a shared emotion,
a collective sigh of relief
and hope

in the strangers standing beside me,
peering into the depths of
the Grand Canyon,
the avalanche of tears,
poignancy, the resplendence of the moment,
the silent connection we shared
in our awe

and in the anguish I feel when a friend has lost a child,
an unthinkable,
unimaginable loss.

Does she know that
my heart breaks
and merges with hers

in this inconceivable
moment in time?

The great secret of our powerful,
magical hearts

is that they are one.

Butterflies

I have seen them all my life,
feeding on the nectar of garden flowers,
in the forest, oceanside, meadow,
in the backyard

in great clusters within the fences of
Butterfly Gardens,
warm indoor zoos for exotic creatures,
flitting from plant to plant,
tiny delicate fairies
mysterious and wildly colorful
like elegant miniature abstract paintings
winged stained glass beings
in search of sweetness and sustenance.

I stand perfectly still
as a butterfly lands on my shoulder
these perfect creatures painted
in intricate design,
symmetry complex
as snowflakes

the Swallowtail
dipped in ruby and gold
accented with panes of deep indigo

The Monarch,
majestic
orange with black stripes
and a cape framed in blue teardrops

It is an illusion that these flimsy creatures,
whose lives could so easily
be extinguished,
are truly fragile.

For no fragile creature could make the
journey from egg to caterpillar to cocoon
to butterfly
with such grace.

Recently, I met a family of strangers in the park
A little girl ran to me
grabbed my hand,
she might have been two,

she sparkled as she danced and laughed,
so full of life,
innocent and open.

I was drawn out of my stiff cocoon
of social correctness
into her joyous, free flowing world
and we danced together.

When she flitted away,
I was left with her joy
but also, with the deep hope
that she would always be this
exquisite spirit,

that she would not,
in later years,
morph backwards
from butterfly
to cocoon.

Connecting With My Parents

Losing your parents is probably the
most traumatic eventuality of aging.
For me, there are the dreams and the tears and
the missed opportunities, the regrets
and the memories.

I have always wondered if my parents are with me.
Do they visit me? Do they watch me?
Do they still love me?

Is this effort to create a book of my poetry
influenced by my father?
Whispered in my ear until finally,
In my 70s, I felt the urge to put my poems out there.
I wonder—whether he is proud of me.

My dad wrote handwritten letters to everyone in our extended family.
He also wrote for a living. He went to school for journalism,
but ended up writing press releases and news stories for the
New York Port Authority. He helped me fine tune my meager
attempts at business writing.
After he retired, he wrote for himself and his family.

In my childhood home, my mom and I sat and grieved for him.

One day, soon after,
A sanitation worker knocked on our door.
He held a ring in his hand, and told us that he had found it
near the garbage by the curb. We wondered how that was possible.
It was my dad's engagement ring, engraved,
lost years ago.

When my mother died,
I found pennies everywhere I walked.
She had always collected pennies,
sometimes bending down to pick them
up from the street, (to my horror) as cars whizzed by.

On my morning walk, a few weeks after she passed, I found a wad of
brand new coupons for a local store that we both liked.
Mom loved collecting and using
coupons!
I called her the "Coupon Queen."

I want to believe that my parents
are letting me know they are somehow fine

and connecting with me in the best way they can.

Mind you, I have a Master's degree in science,
 but there is a part of me,
a childlike part of me,
and maybe you have it, as well,

that still believes in magic.

I Dreamed We Could Hug Again

I dreamed that we could hug again
greet each other with a smile
and a kiss on the cheek.

In my dream I took your hand in mine
and felt the warmth,
the pulse throbbing in your wrist
as I listened to the story about your sister's
strange behavior
we laughed together,
I felt you relax.

I dreamed that I was not alone on my morning walk,
we were all walking together,
so close, our hands were almost touching.

In my dream we were singing a children's song,
simple and true
raising our voices as one,
our soaring song of unity
our breathless song of kindness
bouncing off the mountains
coaxing the birds to join in.
One heart
beating like the graceful wings of a falcon
ascending into the endless blue of the sky.

I dreamed that we could touch again.
I leaned over to wipe a tear from your cheek
and in my dream
our tears flowed together
uniting in a raging river of sadness
winding its way to the sea
where all rivers come together
to become one with the Earth.

In my dream, there was a deafening silence
and in that silence,
that space,

We held each other.

Sunset

The sunset stutters across the domed sky in coral and pink.
It accents the clouds with violet,
like tears smeared in a haphazard, abstract design,
breathtaking,
The mountains reflect the colors of the sky in its rich palette.

You are in another state
you text me a photo of the sunset,
equally majestic, but different in its design and composition,
values of darks and lights.

Still, we are deeply touched in similar ways,
We experience awe and reverence for this moment, for this gift.
We see ourselves not in the shadow of this sky, but in its embrace.

We feel blessed, grateful, beloved, and connected,
the way we feel when we experience the expanse of the sea or the power of mountains,
the depth and mystery of the forest
or the presence of creatures living quietly in our midst.

We understand that the natural beauty of our world is under siege
by the grasping, greed and wanting of our human race.
It is a strong force, but it is not as strong as the peace we share tonight in these quiet moments,
and the power we all share
to protect our world and to love it into safety,

not a given
but a prayer that there is still time.

Ancient History

Best Friends

I can see your straight white hair
glowing in the sun,
both of us
In the driveway of my new house,
in the sticky summer before
Kindergarten
The summer we became best friends.

Neighborhood warriors
running in the tall grass, barefoot,
evading the bees,
scratched by blackberry brambles,
purple-stained fingers and tongues,
faces dirt-streaked,
skinny arms and legs flecked with blood
from climbing trees and
racing through the woods,
its maze of branches
reaching for us with barbed fingers.

We chewed on bitter tree roots
that smelled like root beer
greedily sucking nectar from the honeysuckle flowers
that grew outside our fort.

Spent, we tied our imaginary horses to the bushes
when our mothers called us for dinner.

One day, deep in the woods, we stumbled on a secret:
An old lady lived alone in a small, rickety house,
not yet swallowed up by the newly built homes
devouring our woodland.

Sitting in her tiny, ancient kitchen, heavy with smells of
gingerbread and apple cake,
she read us stories in a thick, German accent.

We often struggled up the slippery sides of a massive rock
in the overgrown gully, sweating as we
pulled each other to the top, red-faced, muscles straining,

and proudly looked out over our domain,
pioneers of a disappearing landscape.

Sometimes, we snuck into the dark bowling alley
that smelled of dirty shoes and air conditioning
to cool ourselves on sweltering summer days

Or ordered egg creams all by ourselves
at Suburban Diner
from the sour-faced waitress.

Years later,
Our woods and gully,
with their blackberry and honeysuckle bushes,
their mysteries and memories,
finally melted away
Like Alaskan glaciers.

The Suburban Diner was still standing.

We ordered omelets,
Remembering, reminiscing about those years,
Jealous of our own magical, unfettered, sun-kissed
childhoods,
laughing about adventures that sealed a
friendship together
forever.

Finding the Child Within

In the cocoon of early childhood,
my brothers and sister and I played together,
sliding down the steps of our two-story house on our rear ends.
We ate the frosting off the Entenmann's cupcakes,
drank fresh milk delivered by the milkman.

We laughed together, told jokes,
made up stories, pretended to be spies,
nibbled shapes into slices of muenster cheese,
Our relationship uncontested,
written in blood
we never thought to use the word love,
It just was.

In summer, I climbed into the backyard pool with my friend, Cindy,
skinny, flat bodies flailing,
laughing and splashing water onto the grass.
In winter, we cut deep tracks,
staggering footprints that left us exhausted
as we trudged our way through the backyard snow,
pants, boots and socks soaked,
feet cold and red.

Warming our hands on mugs of hot cocoa
at the kitchen table

My mother sat on my bed
and sang, "You are my Sunshine."
It was the voice of an angel,
slightly off-key.

It was ok to be me, just as I was.
When I cried, the world felt like it was ending,
but it didn't,
I could be myself, at any moment,

sad, happy, angry, frightened
then everything would be back to the way it was,
my feelings temporary, intense, sporadic
great joy and great sadness
living in a small being
with little experience of life.

One night,
how could I ever forget?
I think I was nine,
A nightmare
that shook my childhood to its core,
nothing would ever be the same
realizing, that night

that everything and everyone I loved
and even I
would someday die

It is not enough to leave the Garden
and to spend a lifetime
embracing this concept,
this truth of impermanence.
Yes, it is the withering of childhood
but it is not the end.

As years go by, I return to my days as a child,
the experience, the feelings,
the strokes of bold color, the vibrant sounds,
the raw, naive emotions,
imprinted on my life
I greet them like a long-lost friend,
with my most tender heart,
my most exquisite compassion
and invite them to join me,
here,
in my grown-up self.

First Love

Sweet summer of first love,
Lying on our backs on the soft grass
Looking up at the stars in the glittering sky,
endless with possibilities and promise,
while the smell of earth grounded the two of us
just enough to keep us from floating upwards together
like lovers in a Chagall painting.

You made me a crown out of clover flowers,
Piercing the stems with your fingernails to connect them.
Our fingers found each other's faces,
Lightly brushing Eternity with our fingertips,
A flash of lightning lit the sky.

Somewhere in the world, there was hate, prejudice, war, death,
but not now,
on this field,
under this sky,
with you.

A moment, a snapshot, a dream,
a flicker in time
before clouds obscured our stars
rain pelted our field
and time moved on.

GH

When I left NJ to go to college in Boston,
still in my teens,
I was euphoric. I was finally a young woman
people took seriously. I was preening my wings to fly
and I was confident.
I was an "intellectual" with a "side of artist," or so I thought.
I also had a wild side.

Boys were drawn to me.
I was inundated with attention.

That first year in Boston, I was introduced to GH. He was on
the Princeton fencing team
and was in town to play against Harvard.
A serious, bright boy from Virginia, we became friends.
He took me to fancy restaurants and made it a point to
meet my parents.

We listened to Simon and Garfunkel records
on a turntable in his dorm room at Princeton,
and he showed me around his beloved campus,
we talked endlessly about our
lives and dreams and our ideas about the world.

The thing was, I didn't love GH, and I didn't know why.
He was brilliant, kind, a Jewish boy with strong values,
and a future in medicine. He was good looking, and he adored me.
It took me a while to figure it out:

He was my father.
He was serious, kind, religious, loyal, patriotic, honest,
smart, and driven,
and close to naïve at times.

While I was a child, navigating my way
through the years,
 to become an adult,

He was an adult in need of being
more of a child—spontaneous, occasionally wrong,
silly,
someone who knows who he is,
not just who he wants to be.

Years later, I met my husband.
It was magical.
We were so different
and yet, something in my heart knew
that he was the perfect life partner for me.

Safety

I remember being five, maybe six,
Holding my father's hand
as we walked the mile to Shul
on the Sabbath,
the painted glass windows in blues, yellows, and crimson
reaching for the sky
warm, dim lighting in the mysterious, cavernous space
but the smell—
the smell has lodged in my bones
all these decades
it is the smell of old books,
the smell of old white men, the rulers of this domain,
each deep in his own prayers,
like tall, swaying trees
rocking back and forth,
tallits (prayer shawls) flowing over
their heads and shoulders,
voices emanating from deep in their bodies, their souls,
trancelike, individual,
and yet a tribe.
I was mesmerized.

My grandfather, Isaac, was the Rabbi in a small, West Virginia temple,
A quiet man, funny, loving, and deeply religious
I remember his spirit, as if it were separate from his body
a warm, caring man.
When his young son, Harold, was killed in the second World War,
Isaac never fully recovered.

When I was nine,
I went to a camp for Girl Scouts
I was referred to, even by the counselors, as the "Jew"
I cried every day, sitting alone in the woods,
until I could come home.

At my bat mitzvah, I was already inching away from
the traditions of my ancestors,
It became clear to me that I was a Jew in a Christian town.
My best friend said in Catechism, they learned that
Jewish people were going to Hell.

I stayed close with my Jewish friends, studying Hebrew after school
at the Temple and becoming active in B'nai B'rith.

I was a senior in high school when
my English teacher told those of us who were Jewish,
"If you don't come to school to take the test,"
(which happened to be on Yom Kippur, the highest of holy days,)
"There would be no make-up."
We would fail.

As the years went by,

I became less religious and more spiritual,
Immersed in Nature, in Life and its possibilities,
I found my strengths in art and music and caring for others,
especially those with disabilities,
I searched for meaning in Love,

Never forgetting my deep roots,
and the feeling of safety
that my religion offered me as a young child,
the mystery
and the goodness.

Spring

I had a friend
We sat in her kitchen and taught ourselves to roll sushi
Laughing and sucking sticky rice
from the wooden spoons
The golden daffodils watched
from their vase by the window,
they looked out lovingly at the sun,
from which they came.

It must have been spring.

We shared stories of our daughters
and their escapades,
they, too, in the spring of their lives
as striking and colorful
as perfect sushi rolls—
orange carrots, green onions,
with a dash of wasabi
for spunk!

Our daughters are grown now,
Young women with burgeoning careers and
sparkling lives
My friend moved on to new friends

How quickly life passes
From one season to the next,
Each season blossoms into a flower,
dried and pressed
into pages of a book

Each season
Its own exquisite,
bittersweet story.

When I Remember You

You were the new occupational therapist
I guessed you were Orthodox because you wore a wig, like some of the OTs.
You said, "no, I have cancer,
but cancer doesn't have me."
I thought you were beautiful.

You were young, newly married,
Every day, you threw yourself joyfully into your work,
always trying to help the teachers, the children, colleagues,
I thanked God for your strength and for your friendship,
For the lessons you were teaching me
About courage, love, hope.

Over the next six years, I witnessed your battle—
It never stole your spirit,
but it left your body ravaged,
you were unable to drive yourself to work.
Still, you came, continuing to serve,
Your work with the children was your life blood,
it kept you alive.

I fastened the beaded necklace I made on you,
Your fine motor skills were impacted, you said,
without a note of self-pity.

One day you stopped coming to work.
Your sister was a month away from giving birth,
but you knew the timing was not going to work
for you.

When I got the phone call,
a piece of me died.

You fought for each day, for each breath,
and when I remember you, which is often,
I think of the shimmering light on the olive trees, the shiver of the tall grass,
the song of the stream, the beauty of the sunrise.

And when I remember you, which is often,
it is because I am thinking to complain
about some minor setback,
some small grievance
in my blessed, precious life,
that you
never
once
took
for
granted.

The Quest for Love

In elementary school, I was invited to all the parties
except those where there would be boys.

The girls who attended those parties
talked about spin-the-bottle
and kissing boys in darkened rec rooms.

In my daydreams,
I beckoned the boy sitting in the corner
with parted lips and come-hither looks,
he would walk slowly to me, lift my chin gently to the light,
and kiss me deeply,
with passion.

In sixth grade,
I pictured the class "James Dean"
on a motorcycle,
my arms around his waist, wind whipping my long hair into his face
our sensual laughter mingling with the crescendo of violins
as we flew past the town pizzeria and the dry cleaners.

On the playground swings,
our feet dragging in the dusty sand,
my best friend told me a harrowing story of blood and babies!
we were eleven,
words from a "special book"
her mother read to her with great import.

We were to accept this
bludgeoning of our fragile childhood,
this mangling of our romantic dreams
with stoic grace.

My first kiss
when I was thirteen —
He was a friend of my cousin's
a homely, exasperating boy with overly large front teeth,
who did not seem to mind my braces.

Initiated, finally,
into the realm of "woman,"
hormones already at home,
wreaking havoc on
my skin, my emotions,
my attention span.

I danced with an invisible partner at night
in our abandoned living room,
and on long car trips with my family,
I stared out the window,
weaving stories in my mind
of a handsome, sensitive artist
who lived in the house we saw from the road
driving through the farmlands of Pennsylvania,
a large tire swinging from an oak tree in the yard,
yellow curtains fluttering in the open kitchen window.

I did marry a handsome, sensitive artist.
He gave me more love than I could have imagined
in those hungry, yearning years

and so much more:
by example,
he taught me to love myself.

Hungarian Food

My mother's parents were from Hungary.
My grandfather emigrated to the US early in the twentieth century
He lived to be ninety-nine,
but he swore that he would never return to his homeland
after the war,
where his remaining family was murdered
for being Jewish.
And he never did.

I have no memory of my grandmother,
only old black and white photos of her smiling,
standing beside my grandfather
outside their apartment
in Cleveland.
My mother spoke lovingly of her mother,
who died too young.

When I was a little girl,
our kitchen was filled with the rich smells of
Hungarian food: chicken paprikash, cabbage stuffed with ground beef,
chicken gizzards fried in schmaltz (chicken fat).

Powerful smells that surrounded me
like a warm hug
and brought my grandmother back to life for my mother
as surely as if she were standing there in our kitchen
in her faded apron,
flour spread over the countertop.

They say that our sense of smell is our oldest and most primitive sense.
It catapults us into memories and dreams as vivid as a Van Gogh painting.

Years later, long after I learned to cook and create my own dishes,
my mother and I joined forces in the kitchen to make wonderful food using
fresh vegetables from my garden: trays of eggplant parmigiana, tomato sauce,
pickles, blackberry jam.

We bonded over many things:
our love of art, crafts, macrame, and tai chi, going to garage sales…

Today, the smell of Hungarian food still wafts through my dreams
and I see my mother's chopping bowl and mezzaluna knife
as clearly as if I were a child standing in the kitchen again,
mouth watering
eyes as big as saucers
waiting impatiently for a taste
of heaven.

This Place

I need to take mental photographs of this place,
this land where I grew up,
this backdrop of multi-colored graffiti,
music, static and sound,
people and animals,
trees and flower gardens
pleasing
like a cozy parlor with eclectic paintings, artifacts and antiques.

This place that saw me through a thousand iterations of myself
as I walked the dog,
or called to neighbors,
or delighted in the evening sky.

This pool I walked to on hot summer days,
to cool my body in the water and then re-warm it in the sun,
in the half-shade of the Sycamore tree, reading
with the white-hot sound of voices and laughter around me.

This place where I take my walk
bundled from head to toe
just past dawn,
snow flurries grazing my cheeks with wet kisses
and resting briefly on the tops of parked cars.

This neighborhood where I dreamed I would live someday,
with its stately, ivy-covered houses
that saw me cry, desolate and flailing in my journey,

That heard me call out to my Divine Spirit
for help to heal my broken life

This place lined with trees that heard my meditations and prayers of
gratitude
for the child who came to me in answer.

This neighborhood that taught my daughter what I could not teach:

How to be a child of the earth,
a friend to fuzzy caterpillars,
a climber of trees,
a keeper of secrets

This neighborhood that raised her to be strong and resilient

The too-small house that we outgrew
and the Dutch Colonial a quarter of a mile away
where we had room to hang our paintings,
make music,
and grow basil in the backyard

Now it is mid-morning and the light blasts through the tall windows of this home
adding stripes to the bare wooden floors,

Empty.

A lifetime packed and shipped

I see this house, this neighborhood, this town
through the damp kaleidoscope of my eyes.
When I dial the kaleidoscope again,
there will be new colors and patterns,

But the light

The light will remain the same.

Hiking with Dogs

It is a soft yellow morning.
My friend Bob and I
travel to the state park in NY
with our dogs.

It is our Friday early morning hike,
anxiously anticipated all week.
On the road, we stop at the tiny market
for fresh dates,
It is our routine.

The dogs are nearly jumping out of the car windows,
straining for their destination,
their excitement palpable
Through the parking area, they run to the mouth of the forest and disappear
into the thick, sun-dappled, stone-laden path,
They wait for us to catch up.

We follow the icy stream, our guide on this weekly journey,
the dogs dashing into the water to romp and chase one another
while we gingerly step on stones, over thick roots,
carefully crossing on fallen logs,
moss thick on the tree trunks
and tall trees looming toward the sky, searching for the sun,
The silence of the forest,
like a symphony of Earth sounds,
crinkling leaves and moving water,
The native animals noticeably missing,
warily watching us from their safe hiding places.

We are trying to reach the part of the stream
where we sit atop large boulders, looking down at a small waterfall,
light pouring into the forest like thick cream,
spilling into the shadows,
but it is not really a destination.

The hike itself is our destination.

The hike was the stream that flowed through our lives, Bob and I.
a shared love of music, nature, and our dogs.
When Talia was born, she joined us, traveling in a front sack and later
a backpack,
Sitting on a rock, I would nurse her.
When she became too heavy for me, Bob carried her on his back,
as she grew, she walked with us
at a pace somewhere between the joyous cavorting of the dogs
and the slower meandering of the adults.
Now she is grown,
the dogs are all gone,
and Bob died a few years ago at ninety-six.
Our unbreakable bond did not.

Now, these palpable,
cherished memories
are mine alone.

Family

Family

Holidays were at my parents' house,
The siblings and their spouses gathering for another meal,
A need to be heard, to be seen, to make people laugh,
clashes, resentments,
possible—no, probable—drama.

Chairs squeezed into every elbow space at the expanded table.
A gathering raucous
and brimming with energy, laughter, teasing, arguing,
voices raised, glasses clinking,

Mom tipsy on a half glass of wine,
while my brother plays Scott Joplin on the piano.
My sister attempting to organize meaning
into our conversations,
which were simultaneously
serious and nonsensical,
books and movies, politics, bawdy anecdotes,
reminiscing.

I carried food in and empty plates out of the kitchen
while snippets of conversations
moved in and out of my consciousness,
like fragments of dreams.
The walls were dressed with paintings all of us had painted
and photos of our young selves
adorned the corner tables.

When everyone trickled
into the night,
back to their own homes,
Exhausted,
I thought,
Please,
Don't
Go.

This is what love looks like.
Enduring another evening of my flawed family,
their clumsy attempts to connect
Leaving me with unspoken feelings, triggered annoyance,

and a glowing warmth deep in my soul that came from belonging to
a family
that would not always be here.

We Had a Station Wagon

We were young
I might have been ten, and I am the oldest
of the four children.

A long time ago,
we had a Ford station wagon, with roll up
windows and wood paneling on the sides.

Just as the evening stars readied
to peak through the slowly deepening blue at twilight,
our parents told us to get into our pajamas
and we piled in the back of the car, thrilled.
We were driving to
Cleveland to visit my mom's sister and
their family!

Too excited to sleep, we sang, noshed,
told silly stories, played games like
"Find a yellow car,"
or a "Pennsylvania license plate."

It was before you could jump on Rte. 80 and drive
straight to Ohio from New Jersey.

The station wagon meandered through
mountains via long, dark tunnels.
We stopped in a small town with a post office, a police station, and a general store
and there were plenty of Esso Gas stations, where we could use the
bathroom and buy Cokes.

My dad sang to stay awake.
It was a long trip,
though I never slept, like my siblings.
Too busy looking out the windows at

rickety farmhouses, barns, silos,
outhouses.
hanging out the open windows to look at cows and horses happily
grazing in their pastures.

We arrived after the sun lit up the
Cleveland suburbs.

I slept on a mattress in the dank basement
with my cousin. As usual, she asked me questions,
and I, with great enthusiasm, answered,
only to discover that she was fast asleep.

I remember that my aunt kept the house frigid—unlike our family, they had
air conditioning, which was exciting, but rather uncomfortable.

We made the same trip each year,
The landscape changed, the highway was open for
easier, faster travel, the rest stops were fancier, we saw fewer
animals grazing in the pastures, more dilapidated wooden buildings.

Instead of the station wagon, we had a car
with an attached camper, which we parked near our cousins' home.
The house was still an ice box.
My cousin still asked me questions while we lay in bed
and fell asleep as I answered.

Good times.
Gone times.
I still smile thinking about them.

Photographs of My Mother

The years changed you,
we molded you,
time altered you
You were painted into the mural that was our lives,
standing out in vivid shades of yellow, cerulean, and pink,
always changing and learning, teaching us, by example, to search
for our true
selves,
I was witness
to your transformations

"Honor your parents"
"Don't talk back"
"Dating a gentile boy after what we suffered in the war,
 is an insult to your Jewish heritage."

Years later, three of your four children married outside the religion,
with your blessings.

I went to the senior prom with a sweet boy.
Later I cried and told you that he was not Jewish,
You were disappointed in me.

Your sons wore hair down to their shoulders—
Yet you bravely defended them to your rigid father.

The world was changing.
Slowly,
you accepted; you grew.

Tall and guileless, coquettish smile, laughing eyes, slim and beautiful,
Posing with long legs and pointed toes
in 1940s black and white summer photos
at Rockaway Beach,

a brunette in an Ohio State football sweater and long skirt,
sprawled on a picnic blanket,
flirtatiously looking up at the boy with the camera,
private first class in the US Army,
my father.

After the second World War,
three miscarriages and four children later,
You became a kindergarten teacher,
a dabbler in the arts
needlework, crafts, piano, opera, tai chi…

Friends and family flocked to you; everyone claimed a special bond.
When they hurt you, you forgave them,
quietly tolerant, accepting,
you perfected listening,
Made it an art.

In the photo of you dancing outside at the wedding,
I see joy and love of life,
I do not notice that you are almost ninety years old

Looking through the kaleidoscope of your life, I marvel at the symmetry,
the endless patterns of varied colors moving, always moving,
changing, catching the golden light…your smile
It took my breath away

You never knew how beautiful you were
Every day that goes by since you left this Earth,
I wish,
with all my heart,
that I had told you.

Garage Sale

Another early Saturday morning,
and my mother waits for me
to drive her to garage sales.

We are lusty pirates searching for treasure.
Maps in hand, she directs me to a sunny yard
where a family's junk is spewed across the lawn
and along the driveway, in cluttered, uncategorized clumps and heaps,
askew on tables or in boxes,
or naked on the asphalt of the driveway.

Dusty lamps, whimsical mugs, childhood toys that belonged to children
long gone from
this home,
Books that have inspired tears bearing smudges of chocolate
on creased pages
or books with curious titles like *Lemons and Lavender, the Eco Guide to Better Home Keeping,*
a contraption that makes pancakes in the shape of hearts— (does it really work?)
Forgotten necklaces with gold beads glint in the sun beside delicate soaps
and vanilla
candles unwrapped, unwanted,
waiting to be re-discovered.

But it is not the loot my mother has come to find.
She collects the smiles, the conversations, the company,
and above all,

the Saturday morning bargaining.

She delights in the exercise of her innate talent as a businesswoman,
a vocation that she sidestepped to become a teacher
And now, deep into retirement,
my mother kibitzes with the lady of the house

and admires the softness of the blue, gold, and magenta patterned Afghan,

Sharing cozy stories of the sweaters she crocheted for her friends' babies
and the macramé classes she took when she was younger, my mother laughs
with the woman while I run my hands over the velvet drapes,
the teddy bear with the cowboy hat,
and the green silk shirt, extra small.

I look back on those Saturday morning quests my mother and I shared
when she was alive,
her warmth drifting across those driveways
to the people shopping in them.

It is spring again as I drive past the garage sales sprawled on the
burgeoning lawns,
spilling out over the yards in riotous color and exuberance.
I smile, remembering,

but I do not stop.

My Father's Voice

My father's voice stands out in the choir,
In tune, but
rough, untrained, not blending,
not mellifluous,
Alone, like a bright red streak
in a painting of pastel softness,

Yet, somehow, I am comforted by this voice,
by this man who put his heart out there with resolve,
without apology,
with joy.

When my family took long car trips,
My father would drive,
and he would sing,
It kept him awake on seemingly endless highways
of monotonous
scenery.
We harmonized together, as a family.
It blended our lives into an ensemble.

My father's long illness took the joy
from that voice, took the voice from the man,
took the music from our lives.

I want to tell him
That I was inspired by his voice,
Inspired by the strength, the love of music,
and deeply inspired to raise my own voice in this life,
to sing, to write, to paint, to care.

My Father's Death

My father was a quiet, serious and soft-spoken man.
He loved to sing,
his powerful voice rose above the other singers
in the synagogue choir.

He loved to make us laugh
but he was deadly serious when it came to his family,
country, religion, and job.

If you were a friend, it was for life.

In a shadow memory, I see him holding my
hand as we walk across the field at Shanks Village,
New York

to a large wooden building overflowing with parents
and children,
everyone sprawled on the wooden floors
to watch a movie.
I was two.

Now, as I drive the short distance to my family
home, thinking about the months—no, years—of
suffering

fear wells up in my throat
but calm rests in my heart.

I knew

My father's caregiver, Marina, distraught,
gathers me up in her arms like a rag doll
a hospice nurse by the bed speaks softly.

A week before, driving home,

I hit a cat who flew out between parked cars
Inconsolable,
I grappled with my powerlessness, as I do now.

My father, eyes closed,
in and out of dreams
of a happy childhood,
his life as a young father with four children,
his brother, killed in the War,
his parents, long gone,

and the illness, which took hold years ago
and splintered his adult life into episodes of elation and depression

to this moment
when pent-up Death traveled up through his body
like lava in a volcano.

I took his hand in mine and whispered,
"Do not be afraid, Daddy."

After a while, I moved to the couch
I do not know how long it was
his body suddenly upright in the bed,

But that was not possible, I thought.
Not solid, more like a shadow,
a figure without substance
His soul?

and he was gone.
the vacuum swept my mother and I into one another's arms
and at last, we cried
in our pain
and our relief.

Visiting my Parents' Graves

Gray stones standing like soldiers in a green field
a city of fading monuments
as always, getting lost in this cemetery where my parents are buried,
this eternal home that feels so contrived,
so cold.

Maybe our last visit,
as we pack up our lives to move across the country

and as always, we find them
in their little corner of the earth
Were they waiting for us?

Always overwhelmed by the moment,
what can we say?
all the things we never said?
all the things we wish we had said?
all the love we feel?

There are no hugs, no eyes to reflect emotions,
no touch to convey what is in our hearts
it is a shadow of a visit,
nothing more
a one-sided conversation imagined
in a foreign space
no more

and yet, our tears glint in the sunlight
our hearts open to pour our love
into the empty space
where memories flow
and whatever shows up
leaves with us
as a sacred message

this goodbye,
as painful as the first goodbye.

Restaurant Reflections

Once again, we are at Little Sicily,
our favorite mom and pop restaurant.
We walk past the outdoor tables,
with their blue umbrellas that gracefully shiver in the breeze,
into the small, colorful space;
Nine tables decorated with red or green tablecloths
for the upcoming holiday season.
There are twinkling gold lights accenting the windows.
A large map of Sicily is hand-painted on one of the walls,
The rest are adorned with badges from friends--police, fire, rescue squads,
framed gifts from happy customers.
Sports banners hang from the ceiling.

We are greeted by the smell of rich Italian sauce and pizzas
overflowing with spices and gooey cheese
and the warm welcome of the couple who run the restaurant.
The husband is busy cooking, but he will come out later to
say hello.

It is Dave's birthday, and he nixed the fancy Italian restaurants
to come here, to this unpretentious, inviting place that reminds
us of warm, welcoming kitchens with family and friends.

When I was a child, my family rarely visited restaurants.
Occasionally, we went to a pizza or burger joint in town with
another family.

The real treat for my siblings and parents was an
infrequent, but much-awaited trip to Howard Johnson's,
where, on Wednesdays, you could get as many fried clams as
you could eat.

We were a boisterous group, telling jokes
and sharing stories,
enjoying being together, being silly.
no one jumping up to "be excused from the table"

I remember that we were allowed to get a cup or a cone of ice cream
for dessert,
the best part for me!
so many choices.
I always got vanilla with candy cane pieces
or mint chocolate chip
and then, I savored my cold, sweet ice cream by nibbling miniscule
bites.
…Everyone grew impatient.

But I wasn't just savoring the sweet taste of the ice cream.
It was the feeling of being part of this large, exuberant,
spirited family,

together for this brief time in our lives.

LBI and the Katz Family

Long Beach Island is a part of my family's history.
In the 1950s,
babies, all of us,
we attempted
to rent a house at the ocean.

They weren't renting to Jews.
Our parents were determined, though, and they found
a bungalow,
Simple,
slightly dilapidated, furnished with dark, musty, stale furniture, no air
conditioning, a torn screen door, and small, but…
Right on the beach!

We loved it.
We left the windows open at night.
The peaceful ocean breeze with its tangy, complex smells,
soft fingers massaging our faces,
the rhythm, the pulse,
the mystery that lived just outside,
captivated us, loomed large,
and was entirely inconceivable.

We returned for many summers,
walking compatibly alongside the Ocean—
a behemoth that transformed itself from hour to hour,
surprising, delighting, and energizing us
with its whimsy, its ferocity,
its shimmering surface,
its powerful presence.

Witness to its many moods:
Bone-chilling rain and cold, wild wind that pricked our faces
and sun that blinded us,
we moved with the sandpipers and the plovers, as they ran

beside the water's edge,
We cheered the swooping gulls and the terns, the seabirds that dove
into the water or floated on top.
We navigated the rocks, the jellyfish and the broken shells
in our bare feet.

As a family, we explored the island and all it offered, the quirky shops
and the restaurants that smelled of salt, fish, and sun,

The Bay—
where sunsets were gorgeous,
my favorite place to swim,
the water rocked me in its gentleness and
carried me with soothing hands to the shore.

My father's dream to open a pancake house in LBI never materialized,
we continued to spend time on the island,
In my twenties, I performed in night clubs in Beach Haven and Ship Bottom,
My brothers were both married on LBI, my sister officiating.
My brother David bought a beautiful condo right on the ocean,
and turned it into an inviting getaway for family, friends, and renters.

My favorite memory though, is
sitting in front of
our rented bungalow
with my sunhat, feet sprawled out
on the sand, reading a book for hours,
as the gentle ocean wind whispered in my ear,
its song
of endless transformation.

Watching Tal Grow

Before Dawn

Before dawn, I ride the wave between night and day
The moon a blazing white citadel lighting my way
as I walk through the perfectly silent night,
a sliver of day pushes its way up from the mountains in the east
with stealth, courage,
glory,
to be born yet again in this turbulent world.

Birds yawn and stretch in their musical way
Owls glide between rooftops
Filling the sky with belligerent and mournful tones.

You were a voracious child
Devouring life with a fire in your soul
to fill your slender body with awakening,
your heart aching for more,
different,
blue, pink, violet,
piercings, tattoos,
new languages
dreams replaced daily.

Brilliance and melancholy,
a helix of great love
and great angst.

and just when I think that you are
finally happy,
you are moving again.

Away from me.

I see through my tears that the birds are finally grabbing
the day
the coyotes are tiptoeing around the oleanders

for breakfast
and the moon has faded just a little

The new day has taken the landscape captive
making shadows, and glimmering off the leaves of the
olive tree.

Soon the music and light will try,
with such love,
To restore my heart.

You Will Be Thirty In a Few Months

In a few months, you will be thirty.
I feel as if I have lived your amazing life
as well as my own.
I felt the same pain, the same exhilaration, the same joy, the same fear
you were living,
but I felt it all from a slightly different perspective,
a perspective I wish I had when I was young, that small distance that creates enough space
to see the whole tapestry, not just the designs that are its parts.
I struggle with that in my own life even now.

I need to step out of my life at times, pause, decide which stories I am telling
myself are real and which
are simply
stories.

You cannot just run away, dear one.
You cannot simply move to another country or to the other side of this one because you like the winter trees.
You cannot simply throw away the investment you have made in your extraordinary gifts without experiencing some loss.
Yes, there are times when change is clearly in your path, but you must choose
when and where and how to make that change happen,
listening carefully to your heart.
Is it a true calling?

Pause. Be the owl sitting on the tallest branch of the tree,
Seeing your life from all angles.

Talya is "Dew from Heaven" in Hebrew

I was told that I would most likely be unable to conceive.
 In the late 1940s, they prescribed DES, a drug for women who
experienced miscarriages—My mother had three before she took the
approved drug,
and became pregnant with me.

They took DES off the market in '71, but not before they realized
that it could cause reproductive issues
in babies of the
women who had taken it.

We still tried.

When we returned from celebrating a belated honeymoon in Italy,
I was pregnant against all odds. I was 41.
We now entered a tornado of feelings and emotions
as incompatible
as "real" and "unreal."

I remember taking a pregnancy test and then driving to
Dave's business office to tell him we were pregnant. He looked
about to faint.
Everything changed. The world was crazy, upside down, confusing,
glorious, and terrifying.

Dave was building a fence in the back yard and remaking
our little house into a soft, safe, foreign home. Nesting,

Pinning names on the refrigerator,
wondering together about this being who was going to
become our family.

I was watching my body morph and eating nonstop.
I was beautiful.

I still hiked with the dogs and sang at the catering halls,
in recording studios, and in my music room at home.

My pianist drove me to our gigs on Long Island.
He drove too fast, but I felt like there was a golden shield
surrounding my body. I was a Greek Goddess with superpowers. I was invincible.
Nothing bad could happen.

I took my walks in the morning, singing songs to my child, pouring
music into my baby's world, choosing the songs
I wanted her to own.

I remember a crabby nurse at the hospital, commenting under her breath,
with disgust, about women who had children at my age.

I shared a room with a seventeen-year-old.
How strange, I thought, that we were roommates, both novices at this,
approaching childbirth from such different perspectives,
different angles.

Both as joyful as two mismatched roommates could be.

Talia, Part I

There are dozens of albums that tell the story,
but the actual collection of pictures exists in our minds,
without yellowing, disintegrating, or getting lost,
accompanied by raw emotion,
laughter, memories, recognition.

Talia was cranky, sitting in her high chair,
refusing again to eat peas and carrots.
In a last ditch effort to win her attention, Dave ran out to buy
Dairy Queen, her first taste of sweets.
We watched her face melt faster than the ice cream,
a look of pure ecstasy blooming there.

I see Talia napping on our dog, Sassy Kat's soft, yellow fur
in the living room of our first house

and naked on the patio, just past sunset,
smoothing Sassy's rump, like
a miniature masseuse.

Running into the yard naked in the rain, giggling,
me, dragging her back into the house, trying to hide my laughter.
She loved being naked.
She still loves the rain.

The first time she ate strawberries, out on the porch,
as we watched her devour the sweet, juicy fruit
that dripped down her chin,
She looked like an escaped circus clown,
demanding more until the bowl was empty.

Jumping into a pile of leaves,
first autumn of her life,
wearing her plaid scarf
and white hat with fake fur that circled her face

like a vintage cameo,
my mother standing beside her with shining eyes.

Lying on her belly in the backyard, examining the grass,
oblivious to all but the butterflies lighting on her fingers.
She doesn't notice me taking the picture,
but years later, I painted the scene in watercolor.

Playing with the neighborhood boys, the twins from across the street,
She loved being outside, hanging with Tommy and Danny,
digging, pretending, making up games.
I took pictures of them sitting
by the vine-covered fence Dave built.

Me, carrying Tal in a front pack, and later a backpack,
as Bob and I hike with the golden retrievers in Harriman State Park,
our Friday morning ritual.
We follow the goofy retrievers up the stream to the big rocks overlooking
a cascading waterfall, watching as they splash and cavort,
all of us
working up an appetite.

Talia took my favorite albums with her when she moved to the east coast,
She loses everything!
Which brings me to the point:

These photos must remain within our hearts.
Photos are NOT reliable,
even online, they disappear,
as do our minds, our computers, our albums—

Only our hearts are safe,
as long as they are visited and shared.

Talia, Part 2
"An Unusual Child"

When she was two, I enrolled Tal in a library program
for pre-reading little ones and their over-achieving parents.
The librarian, a sweet, progressive educator,
was wonderful.
She ran a loose ship, with many degrees of fun,
Learning, and of course,
chaos.

Tal did not sit in the circle on the rug with the other children
while stories were read.
She pranced around like an untamed colt,
a whirling dervish,
dancing to her own inner music.

This concerned me a little, but after speaking with the librarian,
I was assured that my daughter was fine.
We made friends with the other moms and their children, and kept
those friendships for many years.

The truth though, was that Tal was indeed different, and this was
to be an issue in elementary school and beyond.

She read and wrote earlier than most of her peers. When she was nine,
she consumed "Harry Potter and the Deathly Hollows,"
all 759 pages
in one sitting
as we drove to Cleveland from NJ.

She had perfect pitch.
A natural musician, she played both cello and violin as first chair
for the elementary and middle schools and was principal
cellist for the Bergen Youth Orchestra. She was ten.

Talia was bullied in elementary school,
on the playground and in the classroom.
She was different, not everyone understood her creative take on life.
It broke my heart to see this.
I went to the principal.
"They don't get her yet, but they will. Have patience," he told me.

A new student, a seven-year-old, was moved into Tal's fourth grade class.
Maria and Talia became fast friends.
Maria was a genius whose parents were both PhDs in their
respective fields.
Talia and Maria were outcasts,
but they had each other.

When Talia was accepted into Juilliard, the principal's
words became true.
Her peers didn't always understand her,
but they were in awe of her achievements and talents.

As an adult in her thirties, Tal was diagnosed with ADHD.
This came as quite a shock to us.
She was so successful, a high achiever.
She spoke a number
of languages, with perfect pronunciation.
How could this be?

Tal explained to me recently that she had to work harder for those
achievements because ADHD made it more difficult to complete projects,
sit and practice an instrument,
organize her life.

During the pandemic, she came to live with us for nine months.
During those months, before her diagnosis,
I saw firsthand what ADHD looked like:
She couldn't complete tasks she had
offered to perform, such as helping with meals,

cleaning up her space, or following basic house rules, like keeping her
cats off the countertops.

Now, I know what I didn't understand before—that
her life has been more difficult
than anyone had imagined,

This difficulty is not just hers, but also Dave's and mine,
for us to truly understand this amazing person,
and to help her
navigate the roadblocks her ADHD has set up—

to be happy and to become who she truly is:
a beautiful, loving soul,
and a remarkable woman.

The Cats

The cats have come to stay.

Three of them, each a different person.
Zechi is talkative, he looks at me with wild eyes and speaks,
thinking I understand "cat,"
But I haven't learned it yet, I tell him.
After a while, I see that he will move into positions that he favors
to be rubbed, scratched, and stroked.
He teaches me his favorite poses, but I am a slow learner,
I miss that one of those poses will inspire a claw to spring out unexpectedly
and there is a rendering of red marks on my hand
that reminds me
to learn my lesson faster.

Spuds has a stub of a tail that wiggles back and forth—he is part Manx.
I call him the sensory cat because he likes to get into tiny spots
like the bathroom cabinet or the back of the closet,
or the Amazon box that brought me
art supplies last week.

He lifts his chin to my face and brings his nose to mine.
He is a suckler, a kneader, and a lover of crinkling sounds.
He is also a destroyer of chairs and their underbellies,
But I forgive him because he is truly a lover.

Lastly, there is Pascal, the most complicated cat of all.
Pascal was the most abused of these rescued babies.
He stares at me with huge, round eyes and a come-hither look,
But when I approach, he retreats.

I can feel his wanting, his needing to be held and loved,
and my hands long to hold him and take away his fears
with my tender touch,
and the sweetness of my voice in his ear.

I know he needs love,
and occasionally, he will allow my touch,
but then he runs and hides.

I wish it would not be so hard for him in this world
that cannot understand
just how perfect he is.

The Most Glorious of Songs

You graduated from Juilliard looking like a boxer who had gone too many rounds in the ring,
You were beaten before your career had even begun.
"I'll go back to school to become a linguist," you said,
or "maybe I'll teach English as a second language."
Anything not to jump back in that ring.

I remember when you were too young to know how bleak the world could be.
You played cello with your eyes closed and your heart open.
You understood the gift you had been given.
It was all so clear.

Years later, you weren't sure.
Teachers who told their students that only a few of you would make it,
Classmates who failed to achieve and classmates who achieved too much,
You got into your bed and became tangled under the covers,
Stuck.

We took walks.
I talked to you endlessly to try to remind you of the you that glowed from within,
The you that could spin gold out of sound,
The you that made magical stories come out of a cheap cello when you were nine,
Sitting on the stage, looking out at the audience,
with your pigtails and mismatched socks.

You will never know how I bled for you, and you will never know how my heart exploded in the most glorious of songs
when you untangled your small body from that bed,
gathered up your most exquisite courage and your most brilliant trust
and made your dreams come true

with the most solid belief in yourself
and the tenacity to make your beautiful life materialize
from the inside out

Still Learning about Love

Zechi has a rare cancer,
only six cats on record, the vet says.
no information available about prognosis
Thankfully, he is not in pain.

Zechi is the first cat that Tal rescued in Arizona.
When she told me she had adopted him,
I was concerned. How can you take care of a cat
when you are in the Symphony?

When I turned around, she had rescued two more cats:
Pascal and Spuds. Good decision, because the three of them
take good care of each other when she is out and about.

Zechi is the oldest of the "boys." He is ten now.
He is definitely the King Cat.
He is laid back, chill.
When the sun shines through the large windows of Tal's
apartment, leaving sun stripes on the floor,
he likes to bask in the light,
loves to sit on top of the fridge looking down on his domain,
loves to chase elastic hair ties when you shoot them
across the floor like slingshots,
loves to catch the red laser light on the wall
when Tal uses the pointer,
loves to cuddle in a basket with his brothers,
loves to play with anyone who is game.

When Tal says "Zechi, say hi,"
he does just that. He imitates her voice exactly: same pitch, same rhythm.
I laugh every single time,
 "You guys gotta take this on the road!"

Tal paid for the first surgery for Zechi,
Now he needs another one.

Thankfully, she bought pet insurance last year.

Animals live in the moment, in the Now,
I want to take lessons from them on
"How to be fully present in your life."
As far as I know,
They don't concern themselves with what will happen tomorrow.
So why am I talking to Tal on the phone, trying to hold back
my tears.

It's not just that I love my daughter, and I love her cats,
It is because of Sassy, the Golden Retriever I named
after Sarah Vaughan, my favorite jazz singer.

Sassy was with us for eleven years. She started out as a puppy,
but became human over the course of her life,
laying with me on the bed when I went into labor with Talia,
caring for the baby when she was born—

Sassy was family. I took her everywhere with us.

I was so broken when she passed
that I never let myself love another dog with all my heart again.

But I have learned so much from Tal
about loving.

Now, I cannot run from my heart
as my daughter goes through this,

because I know
she will need me.

Rescue

My daughter Talia is a beautiful and kind
rescuer of cats (she has three)
She never walks past a dog without bending down
to go nose to nose.

Thirty-three years old, a lover of all animals,
She tells me that she has taken a nineteen-year-old daughter of a friend
under her wing.

But Diana is not a cat, and she will not be rescued easily.

She has dropped out of college, working odd jobs,
using the money to buy drugs, body piercings, and tattoos.
She has tried heroin and cocaine, and has had a car accident and been
arrested.
I tell Tal that this is someone who needs professional help beyond seeing
a therapist,
that she may need twenty-four-hour professional support and perhaps
medication.

Tal says Diana does not think she has a problem even
though she is depressed and withdrawn.

"Could you speak with her parents?" Tal asks.

I am on the other side of the
country, so I call.

The conversation is tense, uncomfortable.

Two days later, Talia calls to tell me that Diana has a new boyfriend,
and they have decided to
get married,
though they have just met.

When I get off the phone, I feel my tears coming, though I do not know this
young woman.

I am suddenly a child again, playing with my cousins
at their home in Cleveland.
Barbara, the youngest, is cute and funny with a whiny voice.
She wants to play with us, but CF,
her older sister, grabs my hand and pulls me out of the room.
Barbara was always jealous of her older sister.

She did not have a successful marriage.
She lived on the streets for many years, although she had at one time been
a nurse, a mother, and had owned a home.
She died alone in the corner of a public garage, never believing that
she had mental illness that could have been treated.

I think of her often, wondering why
some lives are lost to heartbreak
that did not have to be.

Conversation with my Daughter

Just found out a friend of mine was diagnosed with Parkinson's.
I am feeling sad.

Talia calls as I get off the phone.
She sounds upbeat, so I breathe.

The words don't match the cheerful voice, though.
They paint a different picture:

Her job is most likely ending in a month or so—the company is struggling
and she is fairly new to the field.

"My manager is ghosting me," she says.

Are you signing in for work every day?

"Yes, but they have me doing tedious busywork
that is driving me nuts."

Ok, but you knew this, you are sending out resumes and
keeping in touch with the headhunters? …

"Oh, yes, I am and I am confident that it will work out,
given some time."

Well, that's good!

"I think Zechi has another lump, and just as I am
paying off the $7,000 operation for the last lump!"

oh dear.

"No, no, everything is fine. I will see the vet next
week…"
"It's really hard to work in the apartment, though,

there are now two screaming babies, not just one,
in the upstairs apartments,
both in their terrible 2's
and that sets off the pit bull, who barks incessantly."

Can you take your laptop to the coffee shop?

"Don't need to, my new brown wireless earbuds
are doing the job."

Well, that's good....

"Ugh, I have to get going," she says, "First, I have to stop in to spend some time with Erica's cat, who is dying, and then I need to get gas in the car."

Ok, will let you go, then, Honey.
Everything is going to work out great, you know?

"Of course, Meemee!
Well, Talk soon.
 Hugs!"

How does she manage to deliver all this information, sound upbeat,
and still,
I am left exhausted
and vaguely depressed....

My Endless Love

Davie's Birthday

Holding hands, fingers entwined
This mystery of life
Synchronized breathing, painting, laughing
Taking turns sad, happy, frustrated, joyful,
overwhelmed, angry…
We are alternately caretaker, cheerleader, teacher and student
--as necessary

This year was different for both of us.
I had my first inkling that you were not
made of steel or solid as a horse,
but rather tender and vulnerable
as the rest of us

Not a bad thing to have happened for either of us,
I forgive you for being human, you know.

In all your magnificence, you fooled me for too long.
Now I understand that in some ways, we are equal
When I thought,
Surely,
I was less

In the hospital, you were as tight as a wound-up toy.
I wanted only to be there for you,
Frightened that I would not be enough,
shivering with your pain

Life unfolds in ways that bring us closer
to ourselves
and to each other.

I am proud and happy each day
that I have you securely in my life,
no matter the moods and shifts
in the haboob of our days!

With Monumental Love
On your Birthday, Davie
XXXOOOOXXXXOOOO

Forty-One Years Later

I look at photographs of my husband in the early days of our relationship
He is breathtakingly handsome,
but I barely notice this when I see him for the first time.

I am taking a dance class and he is sitting on the shiny dance floor right behind me,
the only male in a sea of toned women.

I startle when I look in his eyes though,
they are mesmerizing,
wide with fierce, bright energy,
green with gold flecks,
I forget to listen to what he is saying.

I have recently become bored with dating and certain that the story
of true love is not to be mine.
I am 32. This young man doesn't
fit my definition of a dating candidate.
He is 6 1/2 years younger than I am,
like a puppy, following me around with his piercing eyes.

Besides, I am in a sort-of relationship that is at least comfortable, if not consequential,
a sexy musician friend who stops by my apartment every few months
when he is not touring with the Buddy Rich band.

Dave does not take no for an answer.
He talks me into a date.

He takes me to a crowded bar that I absolutely hate. I can't even make it
to the ladies' room—too many people squeezed into this popular, smoky, hip
place.

When he finally takes me back to my apartment, he trips going
up the steps,
because he is wearing fashionable shoes of some sort
that are wildly inappropriate for actual walking.
We end up in the emergency room.

For some unknown reason, I am touched by his vulnerability.
I agree to another date, still unsure why.
This time, I begin to see that he is a
sweet, candid, funny, sensitive guy who seems to adore me in a
sort of Don Quixote way.

It's raining and he carries me over the puddles, like a chivalrous
Knight of Old.
I slowly fall in love.

I get some flak from my brothers though.

They don't see
what I see.

There is something about love that knows when it is meant to be,
Overriding logic and common sense,
Something primal, preeminent, knowing,
Something Mystical

and yet deeply true.

Time has proven me right.

Just the Two of Us

Thanksgiving is just the two of us this year,
most years, actually.
Our siblings are on the east coast or New Mexico,
ensconced in groups of friends or spouse's
families for the holiday.

I miss Talia, but she is deeply involved in
her job,
Too anxious to leave, even for
Thanksgiving.

We always hosted back in New Jersey.
Our downfall: no matter what I prepared—
no matter how delicious—exotic, plentiful, or
enticing,

It was not turkey.

So we celebrate with each other,
A meatless meal and a good glass of wine.

I am excited for Thanksgiving this year, though,
because I have so much to be grateful for: my new vision, our good health,
beautiful home, friends, painting, and enjoying the Arizona
life,
the lantana we grew this summer, which continues to grow and
bloom on the
patio, greeting us as we walk out the door each morning,
the yellow bell, which has dallied the last 5 years,
now, finally blooming with all its heart.
For each other, our family, and for our beautiful, sweet daughter.

There is always something to be grateful for,
but celebrating it each year
holds us accountable for the times we forget

to look up at the ever-present brilliance of stars,
enjoy the blazing pink sunsets
the soft, pastel sunrise,
the violet mountains, the hummingbirds that never cease to
make us smile…

for the times we leave the supermarket with an abundance of
food without feeling incredibly blessed,
or we forget to
tell each other,
"I love you more each day.
I am grateful for you in my life."

For all the times we forget to look up to say "thank you"
for another day.

Love Story

I fell in love dozens of times before I met you
Each time, I recognized that feeling:
giddy, energized, aware.
I was beautiful, delicious, newly born,
every nerve ending lit by a fire
that would not be
extinguished.

But then it was.

I recognized that feeling when I fell in love with you
like the world was opening its insides to me
like time was doing somersaults—
trees whispered and flowers smiled,
bees ceased pollinating to wink at me
drunk on loving you.

What was different this time?
I cannot say
Maybe nothing for a long time
Love is love, right?

But then colors began widening, deepening
what was a soft, light pink became a rich, ruby red,
The smell of lilacs permeated the fall and winter air.

Seasons passed,
pets and parents died,
jobs were lost and gained
friends walked in
walked out
change nudged us, pricked us,
caressed and abused us,
and our love went deeper still.

Sometimes I am sure that I am seeing
straight through to your soul,
those shimmering gold waves.

When I curl into your body under the covers,
I feel the shape of my own body,
my heart.

When the world seems to be ruthless and cruel
I silently reach out for you in the darkness
your warm hand is all I need
to realize,
with joy,
that my heart held out
for the most perfect,
tender love.

Sleep Partners

Sleeping next to you over the years,
Our bodies have blended
like peanut butter and chocolate,
a happy pairing,
a delicious and dramatic combination
that has drawn us closer in
our waking hours.
Not because we are alike,
but because we are different.

You have fallen asleep, with a full cup of coffee in your hand,
(I have witnessed this!)
head hitting the pillow and devolving into unconsciousness,
while I toss and turn like the Princess and the Pea,
shifting, turning, repositioning endlessly,
my brain a babbling brook,
Sleep moving slowly and steadily
out of reach.

When my close friend decided to end our long friendship,
I went through the stages of grief,
finally, anger,
which kept me tossing and turning, mumbling,
then, sobbing into my pillow
and finally reaching out to your sleeping body.
Without missing a beat, you took me into your arms,
brought me a cold pack, water, a banana, and gave me an
incredibly professional massage.

I often reach out to touch you, just to feel that powerful strength
that lives in your warm, muscular body. It calms me.
I am a sucker for being rescued by a Prince.

I would be surprised and delighted if suddenly you reached out to
wake me, to tell me about some niggling thought that was
keeping you up,
but that will never happen.
You are the rescuer,

and who am I to argue?

Arizona

Wind Chimes

The wind chimes have every reason to dance with glee,
looking out at the wide expanse of stone around the house
in shades of brown and grey with
recurrent gold accents,
the violet mountains with their beckoning silhouette
in the distance.

The wind chimes are closest to the old olive tree, who leans in slightly
to listen
to its captivating heart song,
a serenade that coaxes the young orange tree
to grow stronger against the wind
and accompanies the frenzied dance of the hummingbird,
sipping nectar from the flowers
of the orange jubilee.

The wind chimes tinkle in the low breeze, barely audible,
but in the sometimes rattling winds of the desert
they call with abandon
to the denizens of the backyard,
whipping the trees and bushes
into a frenzy.

In New Jersey, my brothers and sister and I ran through the yard
as the hurricane strengthened.
The wind was glorious and exhilarating.
We knew nothing of danger then, in those days,
only that our hearts soared and our imaginations
lifted us from the ground, like Mary Poppins,
and we flew,
untethered.

Did the wind chimes also accompany us as we
ran along the shore of the wild ocean
at Long Beach Island,
the wind stirring our souls?

Yes!
With the wind comes the music
that begs us to dance
to dream,
to hope,
to fly.

Wildness

I am not sitting quietly in my chair,
feet flat on the floor,
as I should,
to convene with my heart.

On this beautiful day,
I am drawn in by the glimmering of the sun on
the leaves of the oleanders,
the sweet, juicy smell of orange blossoms
and honeysuckle.

For me, walking is sensory meditation.

I bask in the beauty that lives here,
The dappled violet mountains standing guard
shoulder to shoulder, with such dignity,
a citadel
encircling this place with love.

Yesterday, I saw three bobcats,
slinking across the
street to the golf course,
entitled, mother bobcat staring me down.

They are exquisite art themselves: dots and lines
and gorgeous patterns
adorn their fur,
pointy ears and bobbed tails--
twice the size of ordinary house cats.
Do not try to pet them.
They are as wild as the desert wind.

These three bobcats are not strangers.
I see them at times, owning the patios and
the backyard tables in the community,

at home basking in the sun
or hunting rabbits.

Once, they caught a rabbit in our backyard,
Tal's cats, visiting that morning,
mesmerized, also traumatized,
They watched the whole episode from the picture window.

I did not.

Living in the desert is living with wildness,
bobcats and coyotes, falcons and burrowing owls,
Javelina herds.

When I venture from my community,
beyond the mountains I see each day,
to the hiking areas nearby—
Cave Creek, Lake Pleasant Regional Park, or the White Tanks—

Wildness increases exponentially.

The Saguaros live in huge "communities,"
Each single cactus plant develops its own
personality: quirky, statuesque, growing multiple arms, hats,
and shapes.
The Cholla, the prickly pear, the spiny ribbed hedgehogs…

So many coexisting denizens of these mountains.

A cornucopia of wild.

Growing up in the suburbs of New York City,
My imagination could not have conjured this
diverse world,
but every day,
I am grateful for this riveting adventure,
This taste of wildness.

What Makes Me Feel Safe

In this upside-down world, what makes me feel safe?

When I walk, plucking a stone from below my feet,
I feel it, both smooth and bumpy,
and I warm it in my hand
I have ripped it from its comfortable, lived-in resting spot,
uprooted it from its home.
Is it afraid?

I hope not, because it somehow makes me
feel *less* afraid to hold it
Maybe it is the solid realness of it, the fact that it is of this Earth,
or how it fits precisely in my palm
that brings me securely into the moment and calms me.
I feel safe.

I am comforted by the mountains which surround my community.
They are from a fairy tale, wispy with cloud halos, surreal shades of blues
dappled with violet shadows
I want to reach out and touch them, but they are not as close as they seem,
Majestic, powerful kings and queens, guardians of this beautiful land,
I feel safe.

When I was very young, I felt safest when I was alone
in the woods or the gully, sitting quietly on the big rock
with my arms hugging my knees, gently rocking,
my face lifted to the sky,
away from the drama of a large family
and the responsibility of being the oldest child.

Now, living in Arizona,
I realize that I have learned much from the indigenous cacti
in their strange and otherworldly beauty.

I am like the Cholla, safe in my prickly armor,
the Turk's Head cactus, blending into the surrounding gray limestone
and protecting its fruits and flowers with dense white wool.

My naked heart is rarely unguarded

and yet,
when I have allowed myself to love
in a wild way, untethered,
like jumping off a cliff into a deep unseen chasm,
once my feet touch the ground
and feel the solid earth,

I breathe,
and I know
that I have never
felt as safe.

Hummingbird

I walked past the honeysuckle bush on my walk this morning
A hummingbird was gleefully flitting from flower to flower,
the sunlight bouncing off its tiny wings, like miniature prisms.

There is a chattering monkey that sits on my head, whispering in my ear:
Planning, plotting, organizing, listing, worrying,
defending, explaining, wishing,
I am pulled in.

Does the little hummingbird, going about its business this morning,
think about what it is doing, should do, will do?
Is it considering what will happen if tomorrow is raining
or if there will be no flowers on the bushes?

I am busy dreaming my dreams, creating my scenarios,
building a future, remediating my past.
In my swirling thoughts,
I am worrying about the election, the state of the world, the future of the planet…

Does the caterpillar dream about becoming a butterfly?
Does it worry about what kind of butterfly it will become?
When it will change into a butterfly?
How it will feel,
What it will do with wings?
Does it care?
Is it attached to its dreams of becoming a butterfly the way I am attached to my dreams?

Sometimes I toss the monkey off my head
Just for a few minutes.
I am weary of my thoughts.
I want to simply be quiet.
When I do this, even for a few minutes,

there is a space for me to be the hummingbird, the honeysuckle bush, the caterpillar, the butterfly,
a space for me to let go, surrender to the beauty and the mystery of my life.

I breathe deeply into that open space.
I feel peace.
When the monkey tries to climb onto my head again, I will not let him back, I say.
But then I always do.

Thrive

Walking in the dark mornings
I lose myself in my thoughts
Today, I turn down Huron, toward home—
It is cold this morning, and I am bundled
and zipped like a present to be mailed overseas.

I smile. There is the Joshua tree I painted last year.
I love to visit that tree, its majestic branches reaching for the
sky, strength and beauty personified.
A golf cart with two barking dogs passes.
The driver barely responds when I say
"hi."
I think he is annoyed at the dogs.

And here is the house I
visit the most on my walks.

The homes here are lovely,
but this house is special.
The entire yard is covered with roses.
Roses in many colors, spread out across
the front of the house and almost to the street.

It was difficult to grow roses in New Jersey,
They were fragile at best
temperamental and uncooperative
for the most part.
They required more experienced and persistent care
than we gave them.

But this is Arizona.
The desert is cold in the morning and at night,
and can be brutally hot in the summer.

It's like seeing the polar bear at the Phoenix Zoo.

How is it possible?!

When I was in my fifties, I went back to graduate school to complete a Master's
in Science. I hadn't been in school for decades.
I remember walking into my classroom
for the first time:

I was that polar bear, that rose.

Everyone looked at me. They were all so young.
I didn't belong,
but I was as determined as the roses
to thrive.

And I did.

The Common Good

When I am out walking in this blue-canopied place
in the palm of the slick violet mountains
breathing in the sun and the wind of the desert,
every leaf, flower, bird, and bush celebrating with me,
a gathering of the most affable,
unlikely partygoers,

the playful hummingbirds
and the scurrying, dancing lizards on the wall,
the cactus that, like a sea monster,
engulfs my neighbor's yard,
a colossal living sculpture,
and the primping spring blooms
readying for their grand debut.

Out here,
Kindness is the language spoken
Beauty is the picture painted.

And here are the ants,
always busy,
always serious,

if you happen to catch them in the act,
always on a mission to provide for one another
to take care
of one another
to carry off their dead
and to bring food to their tribe,
their natural connection.

Like the coyote, who calls for his clan
in a barking, howling voice that
lifts the dawn,
for he has captured his prey

to share,
to nurture his kin.

The detailed order of bees,
workers and royalty
striving for a common good.

There is kindness
out here in this wild
place.

How do I feel when I see the homeless man in the city,
Crouching on the sidewalk,
Alone and wanting of mercy?

How do I feel when I see poverty,
racism,
mistreatment of refugees,
the indignities of our society?

Oh, to be like the ants,
the bees,
the coyotes,

that kindness could be the natural response
to the misery and struggle
of our own kind.

Like the Songbirds

I walk along Deer Valley Road
to see the birds perch on stucco roofs,
on the tops of the lampposts
or on the limbs of the palo verde tree,
its trunk and branches
like smooth, green elephant skin.

I hear the songs…
A chamber orchestra of many voices
They are staccato, rhythmic,
a shout, a whisper
I do not know the names of the birds
but I know them—

Their names are their songs

There is playful piccolo,
frenetic flute,
mournful French horn,

There is a lone voice somewhere above me,
an owl declaring his love in the early morning sky
it is a piercing song,
wild and atonal
impassioned, fervent.

For many years I was the violin, the melody-maker,
belting, brassy,
a flamboyant peacock,
wearing my song like a strapless gown,
a glittering necklace about my throat

Now, I am the cello
the cello is more demure
the cello listens.

I no longer make money singing.
Like the songbirds,
I sing for no reason but to let the world know I am here,
that I am soaring in a magnificent sky,
that I live and love,
that the world,
despite its cacophony,
will hear my heart.

The Little Orange Tree

I remember, before we moved to Arizona,
walking into a yard crowded with fruit trees
the scent of orange blossoms,
a smell more intoxicating than
rose gardens, lilac bushes, or fields of lavender,
more memorable than
the exhale of the street after a summer rain or
the tang of cut grass, green and lifeless
on the newly mowed lawn.

We moved to Arizona,
and planted a little orange tree
in our yard
thin and scrawny
trembling in the breeze.

Each day
I welcomed it
like a new friend moving into the neighborhood,
expecting nothing from it
but survival
coaxing it to drink
and bask in the sun

to enjoy the ancient olive tree,
whose canopy reaches out to cover
it with afternoon shade.

Though rich and juicy fruit will someday
grace its world with vibrant color
and enticing perfume

I am in no hurry.

Too often I have rushed through my life

wishing things to come quickly,
to grow up quickly,
to bear fruit quickly.

Now I want only to slow things down
to merely survive each day
to give thanks for the light, the air,
the water
and the nearness of the olive tree,
light bouncing off its leaves
the tingling of the morning air
and the mellow afternoons of
silence
to rejoice in the smile of the gilded moon.

We are here,
little orange tree and I
we are the miracle.

God has touched us with Life
There is no future
as magnificent
as
now.

Musings 2

Who Would I Be

Who would I be if I let myself be truly open?
I would have a dog again,
a big yellow dog to cuddle in my bed with me when I am sad,
celebrating with me on birthdays and sunny days,
splashing in puddles together,
a dog giving freely of her love without fear and without condition.
I would not worry into the future
about the pain in my heart
at losing her

I would laugh louder, easier
at the waddling quail family, with their funny little hats,
marching over the dry stones,
at my friend's grandson, with his chocolate pudding face
and his gleeful splashing of carrot puree on the highchair,
small fingers orange and sticky.

I would not hesitate to hug the breathless stranger who has run after me
after I left the park bench without my satchel.

I would not censor my observation of the neighbor's "beautiful green eyes"
while we are discussing the weather,
worrying that it is not appropriate to say.

I would not allow anger to shut my heart down
when another is unkind,
without listening to his story
and realizing that it is only fear speaking,
that beneath that burden
is a person capable of great love,
who has lost touch with his tender heart,
for it happens to me as well.

Who would I be if I truly let myself be open?
I would be a person who
loves and forgives herself
as easily and fully
as she loves and forgives others.

In the Light of Day

I lie in bed
listening to my heartbeat,
Willing my exhausted body to embrace sleep.
I crave the sensation of melting into my dream self,
losing my repetitive, mundane thoughts to the wind,
to be replaced by the lightness of flying or swimming or
drifting above the trees,
my hair blowing in my face,
my laughter rising up in bubbles, reaching for the heavens.
I imagine the sunflowers growing tendrils up into the clouds, nodding their
yellow heads, rising to
join me for a cup of sweet tea.
I wish for everything to be trivial, whimsical,
light, silly.
Just for one night.

Life can be so serious.
At least dreaming can be frivolous, can it not?
At least I can unburden this heavy heart for a tall tale of perfection
That I only believe when I am asleep.
At least I can surrender my vigilance to being who I think I am
for a night,
Perhaps, I will be different:
lighter,
airy,
golden,
a new me,
In the light of a new day.

Thoughts on Flying

In my childhood dream, I could fly
whooping and singing,
skimming the rooftops,
to my best friend's house,
perched on the ledge of her bedroom window
like a swallow.

Sometimes, wide awake,
I recreate my dream,
with no excuse except to feel the power, the freedom,
my utter nakedness in the unattended sky.

There is no one gazing up
to see the owls calling each other from the tallest branches,
the whipped cream clouds,
the trees craning their necks to the sun

no one to notice me dipping,
gliding above them
as they walk through the gardens,
chat with friends on the playground,
or hurry home for dinner,
everyone so full of their own lives
their coming
their going.

The first time I flew in a plane,
I was disappointed to see the size of the windows.
"How can I
greet the sun or salute the stars
through these thick, dusty peep holes?"
I thought.
If only there were big picture windows instead of steel
wrapped around this machine

a glass airplane
with no destination,
only the chance
to truly experience the expansiveness of
unbridled flight,
the open, arcane sky.

The solid desert rocks beneath my feet.
Dark, ancient forests
The majesty of towering mountains
The mystery of the endless sea.

While awe-inspiring,
They do not draw me in
as flying does.

I suppose I am most at home
with the birds.

The Stars

The stars pierce the darkness
like pin pricks in a black velvet cloak
wrapped around
the endless open sky.

They speak to the part of my soul that is
Forever,
the part that is sacred.

My dreams fly free,
as high as dreams can reach,
ascending, striving for all that is
Love.

I am a cloud, drifting in and out of shadows
I am a child's wish riding through the heavens on rainbows
a blessing sent to a friend across oceans
a prayer for the life of someone dying in a hospital,
Alone.

I am an owl soaring to the tallest branch,
a noble silhouette of gray against the night sky
strong and silent,
patiently watching the world from all angles
to see our Earth in its unrest,
its angry people,

The fragile planet it is.

When I feel most vulnerable,
most alone on this Earth,
afraid for its very survival
I walk out into the Arizona night

with my tears and my dreams,
and give them up
to the ever-hopeful brightness of the
stars,

before they fade
into the developing dawn.

A Poet Walks into a Bar...

I don't remember writing the poem
or what it was about—something mundane, I think.
I was seven.

Daddy sent it to the newspaper.
I do remember my first bloated feeling of pride, like it was yesterday.
I was a sibling in a family of overachievers,
and attention was coveted—
This was a coup.

That elation kept me going for most of my elementary and high
school life:
Editor of the literary magazine,
Member of a Bloomsbury group,
I wrote a play in French that the class performed for the school.

I was invited to recite my fifteen-minute poem, "We Built our Youth in the Backyard Spring" at graduation.

My first year in college, I wrote a Greek play with choruses.
Good Lord!

Of course.
I was falling apart!
I didn't know what I wanted to do,
and I was trying way too hard.

It was then that music arrived in my world like a lifeline.
I wrote songs and sang with groups, recorded in NYC and LA studios,
Taught out of my home studio, sang at catering halls and concerts.
I was making a living, but not much more.

It was fun and rewarding for a long time.

Then it became a business to me.

When I really grew up,
I wanted to do something more,
I went back to graduate school for Occupational Therapy
and worked with disabled children in the school system.

When I retired a few years ago,
we moved to Arizona.
I began to paint,
an interest that grew out of the art projects I developed
for my young patients,
a lifelong love of art,
and esteem for my husband's artistic brilliance.

When the pandemic arrived,
I was happy painting and enjoying the Arizona life.

Out of nowhere,
I started writing again.
I didn't want to become a poet.
I didn't want to share my everyday thoughts,
I just wanted to write.

I was inspired by Bobby, bass player, dear friend,
who used to make up words when he couldn't find the right ones.
Unpretentiously, he created his own to express his feelings, his joy,
his confusion
in this crazy world.

I thought about that freedom,
that juicy, messy, untamed approach to creative expression.

I wish I could be more like Bobby,

Instead, I write to stop the incessant thoughts that swirl in my head
in the middle of the night,
unable to sleep away my angst,
my heartbreak, or my joy.

I write to make sense of my world
and to empty my aching heart
when life touches me in one way or another.
I write to plead with the universe for peace
or to verbalize the joy that Nature awakens in me,
The sorrow that threatens to break me into little pieces at times.
The awe that I feel to be living an ordinary life,

To be living at all.

When my friend, Marilyn started her campaign
to convince me to create a book of poetry,
I wasn't sure I wanted to put myself out there.
I was intent on protecting my vulnerable heart,

Yet I have learned that I am not as fragile as I
once believed.
After all, I am here, in this life,
in this body, with this heart.

I must be stronger than I thought.

Your Old Eyes

Look with your old eyes at the new dawn.
You have seen it countless times before,
Do you remember?
While you were so busy in those sun-filled, hectic days,
there was never enough,
you were never enough,
it was only a backdrop to your yearning, striving, hungry self.

While you waited for your real life to start,
it was already in progress.

Slow it down!
Now, reach out and touch the life
that has always been here
waiting for you to lift the veil,
not too late to step into this moment with
your old eyes,
to open them a new way
to climb into this breathless, glorious space, this silence,
to claim what you have earned,

to give thanks, and
to offer others the gift

of your
old eyes.

Visiting Donna's Art

My friend Donna is an amazing woman.
I have always known this, but she often downplays her artistry.
If you are lucky enough to see her paintings hanging in one place,
and I hope you do, you will understand.
Luckily, I had an opportunity to visit recently.

Donna's home is a sprawling, beautifully furnished tableau in its own right,
but it is her artwork that generates the vitality and the spirit of the house.
Large, small, vertical, horizontal, her paintings convey light and color to
every room, crevice, and hallway.

I see a large canvas with gold, orange, blue, red, and violet, traversed
by black shapes, drips, and lines.
She frequently uses black in her
compositions for highlight and balance.
There is movement and drama everywhere in this piece.

I am also drawn to an older work—swirls of oranges, reds, blues,
with globes of rounded shapes, and tiny blue accents. "Looks
Mexican," I say.
I recognize Greek, Asian, and Mexican influence in her paintings.

There are pastels, paint pourings, oil and cold wax, collage, neuro-
graphical art
(Incorporating brain cells called neurons, which make an appearance in the
work as squiggly lines)
alcohol ink, notan, (a Japanese design concept that focuses on the balance
of light and dark in a composition),

plus, abstracts and realistic work, like the looming, Southwest scene in her
foyer,
or the splashy orange car she painted for her son, Brendan,
hanging in his bedroom.

Donna is fascinated by shapes and structure in her paintings.
She is an intellectual painter, experimenting with movement and the use of photography, gleaning ideas from unexpected places (the garbage dump, for example)!

We break for homemade chai iced tea and a visit from her sweet,
slinky black
cat, who is looking for a little attention.

Your work is "juicy" and "voluptuous," I say, as I examine an abstract collage with a bulging, textured pink and brown globe, pieces of maps, calligraphy, pale gold, a photo in grey, and tiny stars sliding down the side of the composition.

Donna is a woman who manifests curiosity and ingenuity.
Her home is a palette of dazzling ideas and concepts.
the scope and breadth of her talents, her expertise,
is apparent.
The artist's oeuvre is vast.

There is a large abstract that reminds me of San Francisco, and
colorful buildings sloping up a hill. It is striking, no matter which way
she turns
the piece.

But she investigates every orientation, every angle,
finally heading back to her original choice.

Before I leave, inspired and motivated, we talk politics,
one of our favorite topics.

Besides art, that is.

Mermaid Reflections

I often trade my old wrung-out dreams for fresh.
You can change your dreams as often as you like,
yours to play like a favorite song
or toss into the cold night,
then dream again.

I dreamed I was a mermaid swimming in the water,
light as a leaf floating on the surface.

I dreamed I was a mermaid
wriggling, lithe like a fish
 in my nakedness,

Skimming the surface of the water,
diving for the shimmering gold light,
a buoy bobbing to the top of the warm,
blue water

Reaching for the light, I watch my arms as they propel me,
I feel my toes trailing,
Though I cannot see them,
I know
I am my arms,
my belly,
my kicking legs,
my powerful rhythmic breath,

Thoughts cannot find me here,
I am timeless.

Years ago, swimming in the ocean
Caught in its ferocious grip,
my head scraping the bottom of the sea,
my body dragged like a rag doll,
a piece of seaweed,

the taste of salt in my nose
as darkness pummeled my eyelids.

The gift of surrender found me
and gently left me on the shore

I dreamed I was a mermaid
and in that wondrous openness,
a new dream
formed,
iridescent and intuitive.

Now, I dive deep
to free the artist
and the poet
who patiently wait for the moment
of surrender.

Change

I look up at the stars, fixed in the night sky
Only to realize that they are in fact, not fixed.
Like all the Universe, they are ever-changing,
Moving, colliding, exploding.

I walk in the desert where the saguaro majestically stand in great herds
and prickly pear and sage dot the landscape.
Beneath my feet, the lizards and small creatures dart and dodge,
insects live and die, ancient cacti fall,
A world of constant change
Who am I to believe that I am exempt?

When I was told that I would never regain sight in my right eye,
I thought, no, that cannot be right
How attached am I to my vision,
my independence, my painting…

I am managing, I would say, navigating my loss,
and smile,
(See how brave I am?)
Inside me there was panic and fear, for my other eye, for potential blindness.

As months have passed, I have entered the depths of that fear, felt it from the inside out,
felt its stranglehold on my heart, my breathing, my gut,
wrestled with it, bargained, raged, softened to it,
and ultimately,
allowed it to be.

I surrender, let go, accept what I cannot change.
I cannot fight my own reality,
but truly,
my reality is not so small.

Outside my window, I still see the oleander bushes quivering in the breeze,
the blazing color of the bougainvillea, the muted olive tree,
the quail families waddling by
and the rabbit standing frozen, sensing what dangers may lurk.

I still experience every sunrise with exquisite awe.

Music that Fills my Day

The cats are staring silently out the picture window,
following the birds with their eyes,
their muscles taut.
If I open the front door, they will remain on the windowsill
It is a more coveted place than the outside world—
They are simple creatures in their complexity,
as am I.

Ah, the music that fills my day.
My morning activities are accompanied by the cello and the classical guitar
Except when I am walking
I only need the sound of the moon vanishing
and the sun yawning into the pink and gold day,
the scurrying of the rabbit across the street,
seeking safety from the coyote and the bobcat,
the Arizona irrigation systems waking up,
spitting in fits and starts.

My afternoons are songs,
Songs filled with words and the lilt of voices
Songs that speak to my soul,
that lift my body out of my chair with a throbbing beat,
Songs that cry and bring tears to my eyes in their simple beauty
Songs that laugh for no reason,
songs that rap and giggle, shout and scat.
Yes, my afternoons are a concert of ordinary life
in all its shades and melodies.

My evenings sound like dreams,
harp music that whispers into the encroaching darkness,
achingly pulling at my heart,
bringing peace and gratitude,
memories, sad and joyful
a solitary flute that holds me in its loving grasp

a child singing a forgotten lullaby
in a perfect, piercing voice.

Why must I sleep?
I have no time for silence of that magnitude
If I had my way,
the music would go on and on,
endlessly,
like the sound of the ocean.

www.ingramcontent.com/pod-product-compliance
Lightning Source LLC
Chambersburg PA
CBHW050909160426
43194CB00011B/2334